Project AIR FORCE

W0038660

CHINA'S QUEST FOR ENERGY SECURITY

ERICA STRECKER DOWNS

Prepared for the
UNITED STATES AIR FORCE

RAND

This report, part of a multiyear project on "Chinese Defense Modernization and Its Implications for the U.S. Air Force," examines China's growing energy needs and the measures that China is taking to address those needs. It describes the domestic political and economic dynamics behind those measures.

The study was conducted in the Strategy and Doctrine program of Project AIR FORCE under the sponsorship of the Deputy Chief of Staff for Air and Space Operations, U.S. Air Force, and the Commander, Pacific Air Forces. Comments are welcomed and may be addressed to the author and/or the project leader, Dr. Zalmay Khalilzad.

PROJECT AIR FORCE

Project AIR FORCE, a division of RAND, is the Air Force federally funded research and development center (FFRDC) for studies and analyses. It provides the Air Force with independent analyses of policy alternatives affecting the development, employment, combat readiness, and support of current and future aerospace forces. Research is performed in four programs: Aerospace Force Development; Manpower, Personnel, and Training; Resource Management; and Strategy and Doctrine.

CONTENTS

FIGURES

TABLES

China's two decades of rapid economic growth have fueled a demand for energy that has outstripped domestic sources of supply. China became a net oil importer in 1993, and the country's dependence on energy imports is expected to increase significantly over the next 20 years. It is projected that China will need to import some 60 percent of its oil and at least 30 percent of its natural gas by 2020. This scissors-like gap between domestic supply and demand has forced the Chinese government to abandon its traditional goal of energy self-sufficiency and look abroad for energy resources. China's increasing energy imports are a matter of great concern to both the Chinese government, which seeks to ensure that China has the energy resources it needs to sustain economic growth, and Western analysts, who are worried about the international political implications of China's quest for energy security.

This report examines the measures that China is taking to achieve energy security and the motivations behind them. It considers China's investment in overseas oil exploration and development projects, interest in transnational oil pipelines, plans for a strategic petroleum reserve, expansion of refineries to process Middle Eastern crudes, development of the natural gas industry, and gradual opening of onshore areas to foreign oil companies.

The study concludes that China's energy security activities can be explained in terms of China's long-standing fear of dependency on foreign energy. The Chinese government regards oil imports as a strategic vulnerability that could be exploited by foreign powers seeking to influence China. The United States is currently the most powerful country in the world and is perceived by many in China as uncomfortable with China's rising power. As a result, the Chinese government views the United States as the primary threat to China's energy security, and China's energy security activities, which are largely defensive in nature, reflect this concern. China wishes to minimize the vulnerability of its oil supply to American power. The Chinese government's keen interest in the development of Central Asian and Russian oil reserves and the construction of pipelines to transport oil from these regions to China can be explained by the desire of Chinese planners to secure an oil supply that avoids the American-controlled sea-lanes. Similarly, the Chinese government's efforts to increase its economic, political, and possibly military ties to oil-producing states in the Middle East are aimed at securing access to oil from a region—where the United States is the preeminent military power—that provides China with the bulk of its oil imports. The internationalization of the China National Petroleum Corporation also reflects the desire of the Chinese government to gain a foothold in a world oil market where the leading companies belong to the United States and its allies.

China's international oil and gas investments are unlikely to significantly enhance China's energy security through supply diversification or a reduction of the vulnerability of China's energy supply to American power. Not only is it doubtful that many of the proposed pipelines will not be built, but China's overseas oil concessions probably will not yield enough oil to come close to matching China's growth in net oil imports over the next two decades. Furthermore, most of this oil will not physically enter China as a result of transportation and logistical costs. Instead, it will be sold on the international market or swapped for oil that would enter the Chinese market. Consequently, China will remain reliant on American protection of the sea-lanes for its energy (in)security.

ACKNOWLEDGMENTS

This report benefited from the comments of several colleagues. Guy Caruso of the Center for Strategic and International Studies and Robert Ross of Boston College undertook the formal review. Helpful suggestions were provided by Roger Cliff, Linda Doman, Huaibin Lu, Richard Neu, Scott Roberts, and Justine Rosenthal. The information and assessments in this study are solely the responsibility of the author.

Chapter One

INTRODUCTION

Because 20 years of economic growth have brought China an increase in energy demand that has outstripped domestic sources of supply, the nation became a net oil importer in 1993, and its dependence on energy imports is expected to grow over the next two decades. Some analysts estimate that China will need to import some 60 percent of its oil and at least 30 percent of its natural gas by 2020. The gap between domestic supply and demand has meant that the Chinese government must look abroad for energy resources, abandoning its traditional goal of energy self-sufficiency. China's increasing energy imports are a matter of great concern to both the Chinese government, which seeks to ensure that China has the energy resources it needs to sustain economic growth, and Western analysts, who are worried about the international political implications of China's quest for energy security.

This report argues that China's energy security activities can largely be explained in terms of the Chinese government's long-standing fear of foreign energy dependency, particularly China's reliance on energy resources controlled by the United States. Chapter Two examines energy demand and supply in China, highlighting China's increasing dependency on energy imports. Chapter Three discusses Chinese policies in response to the country's growing shortfall of domestic energy resources. Chapter Four explains how China's energy security activities are shaped by the government's desire to reduce the vulnerability of its energy supply to American power.

Chapter Two

ENERGY DEMAND AND SUPPLY IN CHINA

Concerns about China's energy security are rooted in projections of the country's future energy demand and supply. China's consumption of energy is projected to rise dramatically over the next two decades. Rapid economic growth has resulted in a rising demand for energy resources, particularly oil and gas. Prospects for increased domestic production, however, appear to be more limited. The widening gap between consumption and production means that China will become increasingly dependent on imports to satisfy its growing oil and gas requirements.

CHINA'S ENERGY DEMAND

China's spectacular economic growth is largely responsible for its rising energy demand, and projections assume that fairly rapid growth will continue. Gross domestic product (GDP) grew at a rate of 9.8 percent per year during the period 1985–1995 and is expected to average 6.6 percent per year until 2020.[1] China's energy consumption has grown and will continue to grow along with its economy.

As shown in Figure 2.1, total primary energy consumption in China increased from less than 18 quadrillion Btu in 1980 to 37.1 quadrillion Btu in 1996. It is projected to reach 98.3 quadrillion Btu

---

[1]World Bank, *China 2020: Development Challenges in the New Century*, Washington, DC, 1997, p. 21.

3

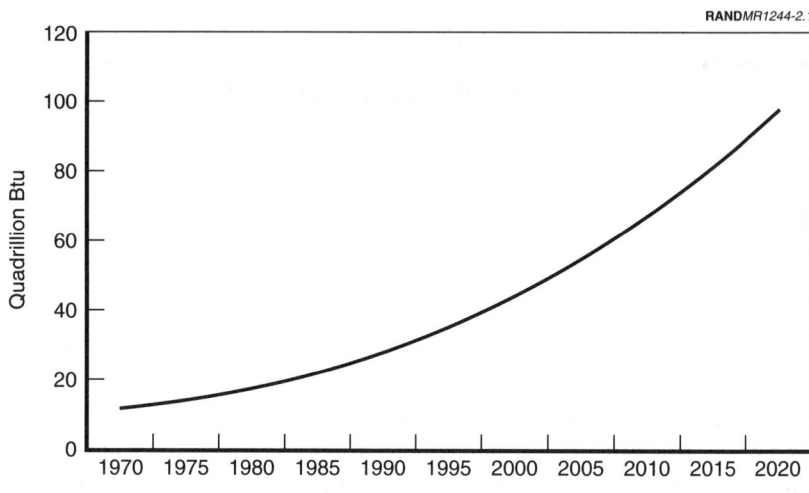

SOURCE: *International Energy Outlook 1999.*

Figure 2.1—China's Total Primary Energy Consumption, 1970–2020

by 2020, which will approach the projected level of primary energy consumption in the United States.[2]

---

[2]Total primary energy consumption in the United States is projected to be 119.9 quadrillion Btu in 2020. United States Energy Information Administration, *International Energy Outlook 1999 (IEO99)*, Washington, DC: Government Printing Office, April 1999, p. 141; United States Energy Information Administration, "China: An Energy Sector Overview," www.eia.doe.gov, October 1997. The *IEO99* projections cited in this report are those for the reference case for China, which assumes an average annual economic growth rate of 6.7 percent for the period 1995–2020. *IEO99* also includes a high economic growth case and a low economic growth case. Projections for the low economic growth case assume an average annual economic growth rate of 3.8 percent. Projections for the high economic growth case assume an average annual economic growth rate of 8.1 percent. *IEO99*, p. 17. It should be noted, however, that there is major uncertainty regarding the measurement of China's GDP and its impact on energy demand. Projections of future energy demand may be inflated because of overestimates of China's economic growth. For evidence that China's statistical authorities have overestimated past growth rates, see Angus Maddison, *Chinese Economic Performance in the Long Run*, Paris: Organization for Economic Cooperation and Development, 1998; and Ren Rouen, *China's Economic Performance in an International Perspective*, Paris: Organization for Economic Cooperation and Development, 1997.

As China's economy continues to grow, its demand for all sources of energy, notably oil and natural gas, will increase. Oil demand is projected to grow at an average annual rate of 3.8 percent during the period 1996–2020, increasing consumption from 3.5 million barrels per day (mb/d) to 8.8 mb/d (see Figure 2.2). However, the share of oil in China's primary energy consumption will remain around 20 percent, partly because of the Chinese government's effort to expand natural gas production and consumption.[3] Natural gas demand is expected to grow at an average annual rate of 11.7 percent over the same period, increasing consumption from 0.7 to 9.5 trillion cubic feet (tcf). China's demand for natural gas is growing more rapidly than that for other sources of energy, with the result that natural gas is expected to grow from 2 percent of China's energy consumption in 1996 to 11 percent in 2020.[4] Increased natural gas consumption is largely responsible for the projected decline in the use of coal from 73 percent to 65 percent of energy consumption between 1996

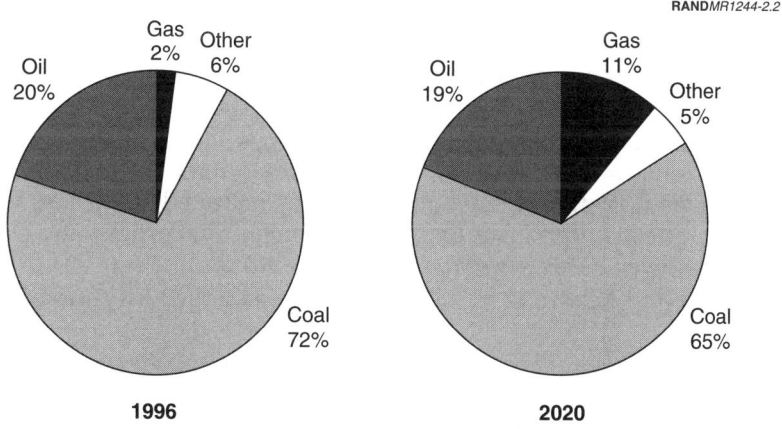

SOURCE: United States Energy Information Administration.

Figure 2.2—Primary Energy Consumption in China, 1996 and 2020

---

[3]*IEO99*, pp. 141 and 145.

[4]*IEO99*, pp. 141 and 146.

and 2020, although demand for coal is expected to grow at an average annual rate of 3.6 percent during this period.[5] Demand for nuclear energy and renewable sources of energy also is projected to increase, but those sources will likely remain a tiny fraction of primary energy consumption because of financial, technological, and ecological constraints.[6]

CHINA'S ENERGY SUPPLY

Domestic resources will not be able to meet China's rising demand for energy in general and oil and gas in particular. Although China is rich in energy resources on an absolute basis, it is poorly endowed on a per capita basis. China's vast coal reserves will continue to provide most of its energy well into the foreseeable future. The nation's oil and natural gas supply, however, will increasingly be unable to satisfy demand.

China's oil supply situation is precarious. China has proven oil reserves of 24 billion barrels (bb), which constitute just 2.3 percent of the world total for a country with 22 percent of the world's population.[7] Estimates of China's potential reserves are highly speculative. Figures provided by the Chinese government are suspected to be artificially high to attract foreign investment, while those offered by oil companies may be artificially low to strengthen their bargaining position vis-à-vis the Chinese government. Scattered evidence suggests an industry consensus of around 68 bb for total proven and potential reserves. This estimate includes 39 bb for onshore reserves and 29 bb for offshore reserves, divided between the East China Sea

---

[5]*IEO99*, pp. 141 and 147.

[6]Demand for nuclear energy is projected to grow at an average annual rate of 9.2 percent between 1996 and 2020, and its share of primary energy consumption is expected to increase from 0.3 percent in 1996 to 1.1 percent in 2020. Demand for renewable sources of energy is projected to grow at an average annual rate of 3.2 percent over the same period, and that share of primary energy consumption is expected to remain around 5 percent. *IEO99*, pp. 141, 145–149.

[7]British Petroleum Company, *BP Statistical Review of World Energy*, London, 1998, p. 4.

(12 bb), the South China Sea (including the Taiwan Strait) (8 bb), the Yellow Sea (4.5 bb), and the Bohai Gulf (4.5 bb).[8]

China's growing demand for oil production is exacerbated by the fact that the major oil fields in eastern China, which account for about 90 percent of total crude production, have peaked and are in decline. Furthermore, efforts to develop both offshore reserves and the Tarim Basin in Xinjiang Uighur Autonomous Region have proved disappointing. Offshore production for 1996 was around 7.3 million barrels, only 10 percent of total output at a cost more than double that of onshore wells.[9] The potential profitability of oil exploration in the Tarim Basin, once likened to Saudi Arabia, is being seriously questioned. Investment is declining because of the failure of both Chinese and foreign companies to make the kind of discovery that would confirm the basin, which has proven reserves of only 1.5 bb, as a major oil source.[10] Nonetheless, China's oil production is projected to grow somewhat over the next two decades, increasing from 3.1 mb/d in 1996 to 3.6 mb/d in 2020. This growth in production, however, will not be able to keep pace with consumption, which is projected to increase from 3.5 mb/d to 8.8 mb/d over the same period.[11]

China's natural gas supply is more limited than oil. Proven gas reserves are listed as 41 trillion cubic feet, 0.8 percent of the world total.[12] These reserves are largely undeveloped as a result of policies based on the view that natural gas exploration and production are subordinate to oil exploration and production as well as a lack of investment, infrastructure, and technology. However, environmental concerns, chronic energy imbalances and shortages, and rising petroleum imports have motivated the Chinese government to de-

---

[8]These estimates exclude areas defined by China as part of the continental shelf jurisdiction but not treated as such by the UN Law of the Sea Treaty. Disputed areas in the South China Sea are also excluded. Mamdouh G. Salameh, "China, Oil and the Risk of Regional Conflict," *Survival*, Vol. 37, No. 4, Winter 1995–1996, p. 134.

[9]Nicolas Becquelin, "The Oil Industry in China Since the Reforms of the Open Door Policy," *China Perspectives*, No. 9, January/February 1997, p. 24.

[10]Pamela Yatsko, "Oh Well, China's Tarim Basin Is Proving a Big Disappointment," *Far Eastern Economic Review*, 19 September 1996, pp. 68–69.

[11]*IEO99*, pp. 145 and 201.

[12]British Petroleum Company, p. 20.

velop its natural gas reserves. Most of China's natural gas is currently used for industrial purposes, but the share used for power generation and residential cooking and heating is expected to expand significantly. Natural gas production in China is projected to increase from 654.6 billion cubic feet in 1995 to 3.8 trillion cubic feet in 2020, with demand expected to increase from 654.6 billion cubic feet in 1995 to 5.5 trillion cubic feet in 2020.[13]

CHINA'S ENERGY IMPORT REQUIREMENTS

The widening gap between China's oil supply and demand and the projected gap between natural gas supply and demand mean that China will be increasingly reliant on imported oil and gas. As shown in Figure 2.3, the shortfall between oil consumption and production was 400,000 barrels per day in 1996 and is projected to grow to

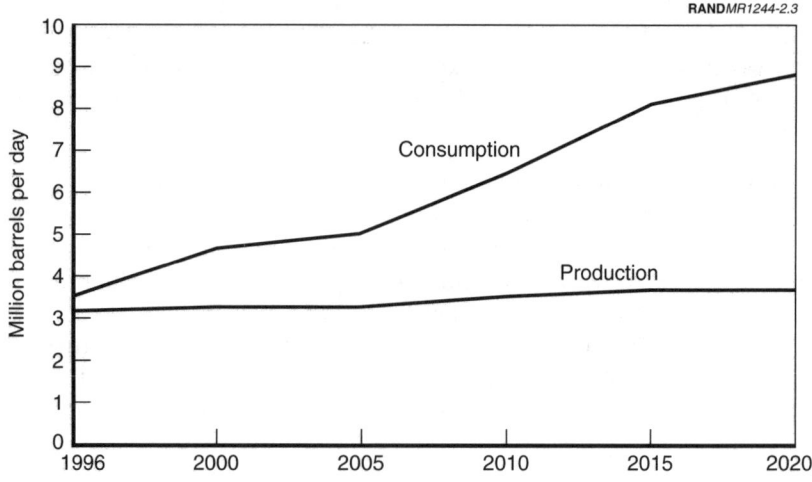

SOURCE: *International Energy Outlook 1999.*

Figure 2.3—China's Demand for Oil Imports

---

[13]Cambridge Energy Research Associates.

around 5.2 mb/d in 2020.[14] Without new discoveries, this means that China's oil import dependence will increase from around 11 percent in 1996 to almost 60 percent in 2020.[15] China is projected to begin importing natural gas around 2005. The share of imports in China's natural gas consumption is expected to be at least 30 percent by 2020.[16] Without the discovery of substantial new reserves or a decision by the Chinese government to backtrack from its policy of market reform and restrict imports, these statistics indicate that China's reliance on foreign sources of oil and gas will grow over the next two decades.

---

[14]*IEO99*, pp. 145 and 201; United States Energy Information Administration, *International Energy Outlook 1998 (IEO98)*, Washington, DC: Government Printing Office, April 1998, p. 175.

[15]These calculations are derived from *IEO98* and *IEO99*.

[16]Cambridge Energy Research Associates. This statistic does not include liquefied natural gas (LNG) imports. Given the Chinese government's recent decision to begin importing LNG around 2005, this number may increase.

Chapter Three

CHINA'S ENERGY SECURITY ACTIVITIES

China's growing dependency on foreign energy is both a theoretical and a practical challenge for China's energy planners. From a theoretical perspective, reliance on imported oil arguably violates the Maoist doctrine of self-reliance (*zili gengsheng*), the guiding principle for economic development in the 1960s and 1970s. Self-reliance does not mean "total independence," but rather refers to the ability to "keep the initiative in one's own hands."[1] Applied to the energy sector, self-reliance implies ultimate control by the government over the domestic energy system.[2]

Self-reliance in oil became the primary objective of energy policy after the Sino-Soviet split in 1960 and the withdrawal of Soviet advisers from China's oil sector. Soviet advisers played a principal role in Chinese energy development in the 1950s, and their abrupt departure delayed and in some cases seriously damaged the large-scale projects they had been overseeing. Furthermore, China, dependent on the Soviet Union for more than 50 percent of its critical refined oil products, out of necessity continued to import those products from the Soviet Union following the split. The loss of Soviet assistance combined with the Great Leap Forward–induced economic collapse created energy supply shortages. China's leaders blamed the entire crisis on the Soviet Union and called for an accelerated effort to be-

---

[1] Kenneth Lieberthal, *Governing China: From Revolution to Reform*, New York: W. W. Norton & Company, 1995, pp. 76–77.

[2] Kim Woodward, *The International Energy Relations of China*, Stanford, CA: Stanford University Press, 1980, p. 33.

come self-sufficient in oil.[3] China's unhappy experience with the Soviet Union has contributed to the suspicion, still prevalent among some of China's leaders today, that its dependence on oil imports and foreign involvement in China's oil sector are dangerous.[4]

From a practical standpoint, China shifted from a net oil exporter to a net oil importer in 1993. China had also been a net oil importer in the 1950s and early 1960s, receiving the bulk of its imports from the Soviet Union. However, the discovery of the Daqing oil field in 1959 and the withdrawal of Soviet advisers from China's oil industry in 1960 enabled China to become self-sufficient in oil by the mid-1960s. China began to export small amounts of oil in 1970. Throughout the 1970s and 1980s, China adhered to a policy of petroleum-led export growth, which involved suppressing the supply of oil available on the domestic market. This policy had begun to take its toll on the economy by the mid-1980s, and the government decided to relinquish the goal of oil self-sufficiency in 1986. During the following decade, as a result of market reform and the consequent rapid economic growth, oil demand increased sharply.[5]

China's recent shift from an oil exporter to an oil importer has renewed concerns within China about energy security. Forty years ago, the Chinese government was worried about China's dependence on foreign oil, but at that time a clear solution to China's foreign energy dependency existed—the development of domestic resources. Barring the unlikely discovery of substantial new reserves, this option is no longer available to China. The reality of increasing oil imports has prompted fears to resurface about dependence on foreign oil. Oil is no longer a source of international political influence for Beijing, but rather a source of vulnerability that could subject China to unwanted foreign pressures. As a result, a debate about the future direction of China's oil policy has been raging within the State Council for many years. China's leaders have been divided over whether China should increase the development of domestic re-

---

[3]Woodward, pp. 32–33, 50–53.

[4]Paul McDonald, "China: is the 'open door' about to close?" *World Today*, Vol. 57, No. 7, July 1995, p. 146.

[5]Gaye Christoffersen, "China's Intentions for Russian and Central Asian Oil and Gas," *NBR Analysis*, Vol. 9, No. 2, March 1998, p. 6.

serves and resist a return to dependence on foreign oil or explore for oil abroad.[6] Both sides of this debate are reflected in China's efforts to ensure energy security in general, and oil security in particular. These efforts include investment in overseas oil exploration and development projects, discussions about the feasibility of several transnational oil and gas pipelines, plans to establish a strategic petroleum reserve, construction of refineries capable of handling crude oil from the Middle East, development of the natural gas industry, and the gradual opening of onshore areas to foreign companies for exploration and development.

INVESTMENT IN OVERSEAS OIL PROJECTS

To improve China's energy security, the country's state-owned oil companies are investing in overseas oil exploration and development projects. The decision to search for oil abroad has resulted from rising oil consumption, declining production, and the failure to make major new discoveries. Another factor contributing to overseas expansion is the peculiar structure of China's oil industry.

During the 1980s, the Chinese government created three large oil companies, each in charge of an industry sector. The China National Offshore Oil Corporation (CNOOC), founded in 1982, controlled most of the offshore oil business. The China National Petrochemical Corporation (Sinopec), established in 1983, was responsible for refining and marketing. The China National Petroleum Corporation (CNPC), created from the Ministry of Petroleum Industry in 1988, was responsible for exploration and production onshore and in the shallow offshore areas.[7]

---

[6]Christoffersen, p. 7; "Energy: The New Oil Frontier," *China News Analysis*, No. 1611, 1 June 1998, pp. 7–8.

[7]In 1998, the Chinese government reorganized CNPC and Sinopec to create two vertically integrated oil companies. CNPC transferred some of its oil fields to Sinopec, and Sinopec transferred some of its refineries to CNPC. However, CNPC is still China's dominant upstream oil company and Sinopec is still China's dominant downstream company. For information about this reorganization, see Katherine Stephan, "Big Gusher," *China Trade Report*, Vol. 36, June 1998; and Fereidun Fesharaki and Kang Wu, "Revitalizing China's Petroleum Industry through Reorganization: Will it Work?" *Oil & Gas Journal*, 10 August 1998.

Division of the oil industry along sectoral lines prompted internal competition between the companies for state funding and for the prices of crude oil, refined products, and petrochemicals. The Chinese government maintained a two-tiered pricing system that required CNPC to sell most of its oil to Sinopec and other industrial consumers at a state-controlled (first-tier) price that was a fraction of the open-market price. This practice left CNPC with limited funds for investment in exploration activities. As a result, domestic production stagnated and imports soared.[8]

In 1933, the Chinese government responded to this situation by gradually relaxing oil price controls to provide more money to CNPC for oil-field development. The first-tier price for crude increased in 1996 and 1997,[9] resulting in enormous windfall profits for CNPC. The value of CNPC's total output reportedly tripled from about $6 billion in 1993 to about $21 billion in 1997.[10] CNPC officials knew that if they did not invest this money quickly, it would be confiscated by the central government. The company was initially divided about whether to invest domestically or overseas. However, uncertainty about prospects for domestic development, the ready availability of oil abroad, and the appointment of the internationally minded Zhou Yongkang as the company's president in 1996 prompted CNPC to invest overseas.[11]

The Chinese government supported CNPC's involvement in international exploration and development. Although the company's autonomy has increased over the years, China's Communist Party and state leadership still choose the company's top management and have a direct say in how the company operates. Furthermore, China's fragmented, bureaucratic authority structure requires the enthusiastic support of at least one top leader for large projects to be approved.[12]

---

[8]Christoffersen, p. 12.

[9]Christoffersen, pp. 13–14.

[10]Trish Saywell and Ahmed Rashid, "Innocent Abroad," *Far Eastern Economic Review,* 26 February 1998, p. 50.

[11]Christoffersen, p. 14.

[12]Kenneth Lieberthal and Michel Oksenberg, *Policy Making in China: Leaders, Structures, and Processes,* Princeton: Princeton University Press, 1998, p. 30.

CNPC began investing abroad in the early 1990s. The company's initial overseas activities were designed to minimize risk, largely because of their limited funds and lack of experience in overseas exploration and production. It focused on small projects such as enhanced oil recovery from older fields and purchases of shares and operating rights in targeted blocks. CNPC purchased reserves in Canada in 1992, signed a production-sharing contract in Thailand, successfully bid to improve oil recovery at a Peruvian field in 1993, and signed an agreement to explore oil in central Papua New Guinea in 1994.[13] CNOOC also undertook its first overseas investment in Indonesia in 1993. The company acquired a 32.58 percent interest in a block in the Straits of Malacca through the purchase of shares from Arco. CNOOC purchased an additional 6.93 percent interest in 1995 to become the majority shareholder.[14]

Although these early investments did not substantially change China's oil supply situation, they did expose China to the international oil business, paving the way for larger future investments. In 1997, CNPC pledged over $8 billion for oil concessions in Kazakhstan, Venezuela, Iraq, and Sudan. The high bids offered by CNPC for the fields in Kazakhstan and Venezuela and the company's exploitation of politically favorable circumstances to win deals in Iraq and Sudan highlighted the Chinese government's growing concern about energy security.

In June 1997, CNPC acquired a 60 percent share in Kazakhstan's Aktyubinskmunaigaz Production Association, which controls three large oil fields in northwestern Kazakhstan (Zhanazhol, Kenkiyak One, and Kenkiyak Two) with combined recoverable reserves of 1 bb. CNPC pledged to invest $4.3 billion over a 20-year period, including $585 million between 1998 and 2003.[15] The company also agreed to guarantee the pensions and housing of some 5000 employees, service Aktyubinskmunaigaz's debts of $71 million, invest $10 million in environmental protection measures, and pay royalties to

---

[13]"China Stepping Up Foreign E&P Investment as Imports Soar," *Oil & Gas Journal*, 9 May 1994, p. 58.

[14]Zhang Yirong, "China Quickens Its Pace of Overseas Oil Operation," *China Oil & Gas*, Vol. 4, No. 3, September 1997, p. 174.

[15]"China Takes Control of Kazakhstan's Aktyubinsk," *East European Energy Report*, No. 69, 24 June 1997, p. 16.

the government of Kazakhstan.[16] The key to CNPC's success in beating out Texaco, Amoco, and Russia's Yujnimost for the tender were two offers the other companies could not match. CNPC agreed to pay up-front a $320 million bonus to the cash-strapped Kazakh government and to conduct a feasibility study on the construction of an 1800-mile pipeline from the Aktyubinsk fields to western China, estimated to cost $3.5 billion, which would provide Kazakhstan with a non-Russian export line.[17] In August 1999, the company shelved its plans for this pipeline, as discussed in the next section.

In September 1997, CNPC offered similar benefits to defeat a joint bid from Petronas and Unocal and another from Amoco to win a controlling interest in Uzen, Kazakhstan's second largest oil field, with reserves of 1.5 bb. In this deal, CNPC paid an up-front bonus of $52 million in addition to an immediate investment of $400 million.[18] Projected total investments by CNPC range from $1.3 billion to $4.38 million.[19] CNPC also agreed to pay 8 percent of its net profits in royalties to the Kazakh government, assume Uzen's $6 million debt, invest $10 million in training programs for oil technicians, and provide $27 million in social services.[20] The key to CNPC's success in this deal was its offer to invest in a pipeline from Uzen to the Aktyubinsk fields. The company reportedly also offered to invest $1.1 billion in the construction of a pipeline from Uzen to Iran via Turkmenistan, which would provide Kazakhstan with a Persian Gulf outlet for its oil.[21] This pipeline is also unlikely to be constructed.

---

[16]Sharon Behn, "CNPC Deal Tops $4 Billion," *Platt's Oilgram News*, Vol. 75, No. 108, 5 June 1997, p. 1; David B. Ottaway and Dan Morgan, "China Pursues Ambitious Role in Oil Market," *Washington Post*, 26 December 1997, p. 1.

[17]Anthony Davis, "China/Kazakhstan—Strategic Oil Deal Recently Completed," *Jane's Intelligence Review*, Vol. 4, No. 12, 1 December 1997, p. 9. CNPC committed only to a feasibility study of the proposed pipeline from Kazakhstan to China, although both parties and the media have portrayed the agreement as a Chinese commitment to finance and construct the pipeline. Laurent Ruseckas, "State of the Field Report: Energy and Politics in Central Asia and the Caucasus," http://204.201.190.101/products/aareview/Vol1/No2/essay1.html.

[18]Davis, p. 9.

[19]Davis, p. 9; Sharon Behn, "China, Kazakhstan Sign Deal for Huge Uzen Field," *Platt's Oilgram News*, Vol. 75, No. 186, 25 September 1997, p. 1.

[20]Ahmed Rashid and Trish Saywell, "Beijing Gusher, China Pays Hugely to Bag Energy Supplies Abroad," *Far Eastern Economic Review*, 26 February 1998, p. 48.

[21]Behn, "China, Kazakhstan Sign Deal for Huge Uzen Field," p. 1.

CNPC similarly outbid larger oil companies for two marginal fields in Venezuela in June 1997. The company offered twice as much as its closest competitors, acquiring the Caracoles field for $241 million and the Intercampo unit for $118 million. Although both fields are producing only small amounts of oil, they could yield more with more advanced technology.[22] The Caracoles field, producing 2,700 b/d at the time of purchase, has an estimated potential for 50,000 b/d. The Intercampo unit also has a substantial upside.[23]

In its Sudanese and Iraqi deals, CNPC combined its deep pockets with political opportunism to win concessions. The U.S. congressional ban on business dealings with countries accused of supporting terrorism gave CNPC the opportunity to replace the U.S. firm Occidental Petroleum in an oil and pipeline project in Sudan.[24] In March 1997, CNPC formally acquired a 40 percent stake in the Greater Nile Petroleum Operating Company (GNPOC) consortium to explore for oil in Sudan's Heglig and Unity fields and construct a 940-mile pipeline from the fields to Marsa al-Bashair, a terminal located near Port Sudan on the Red Sea. CNPC's partners in this venture are Malaysia's state-owned company, Petronas (30 percent); the National Oil Company of Sudan (5 percent); and the Canadian firm Talisman Energy Company (25 percent).[25] The Heglig and Unity fields could contain 8.5 bb to 12.5 bb of oil in place. The pipeline was constructed between May 1998 and May 1999, with 70 percent of the work done by the CNPC-owned China Petroleum Engineering and Construction Corporation.[26] On 30 August 1999, the first tanker from China's concession left Sudan with 80,000 tons of crude oil bound for the Shell Singapore refineries. China has invested over $700 million in the Sudan project to date.[27] CNPC is also assisting in

---

[22]Jane Knight, "The Bids Aren't Marginal on Day 2 in Venezuela," *Platt's Oilgram News*, Vol. 75, No. 107, p. 1; David Holley, "China's Thirst for Oil Fuels Competition," *Los Angeles Times*, 28 July 1997, p. 1.

[23]"China Leaps on to Global Oil Production Stage," *Petroleum Intelligence Weekly*, www.piwpubs.com, 9 June 1997.

[24]Ottaway and Morgan, p. 1.

[25]"Sudan Deal Signed by Arakis, Government, and Partners," *Platt's Oilgram News*, Vol. 75, No. 43, 4 March 1997, p. 1. The Talisman Energy Company of Canada acquired Arakis in March 1998.

[26]"Sudan Pipeline Operational," *Petroleum Economist*, 26 August 1999, p. 15.

[27]"China Exports Oil from Sudan Project," www.chinaonline.com, 3 September 1999.

the construction of a 50,000 b/d refinery near Khartoum, which is expected to be operational by mid-2000 and will use crude from the GNPOC pipeline.[28]

In June 1997, a consortium of Chinese oil companies represented by CNPC and China North Industries Corporation (NORINCO), an ordnance production conglomerate and major arms sales agent, signed a 22-year production-sharing contract with Iraq to develop half of the al-Ahdab field after UN sanctions against Baghdad are lifted.[29] Al-Ahdab, located about 40 miles south of al-Kut in central Iraq, is the country's second largest oil field, with estimated recoverable reserves of 1.4 bb and a peak production potential of 90,000 b/d. CNPC and NORINCO have formed a new company, al-Waha, to develop this field. Development and operational costs are expected to be around $1.3 billion. CNPC has also been negotiating for rights to develop three other Iraqi oil fields—Halfaya, Luhais, and Suba—and to explore the remote Western Desert.[30]

China's state-owned oil companies have similarly sought to take advantage of U.S. sanctions against Iran. A number of projects are reportedly under review.[31] CNOOC is interested in several onshore projects, but no agreements have been signed.[32]

Chinese analysts indicate that China's overseas oil projects are intended to enhance China's energy security in several ways. These investments are not only meant to fill the gap between domestic oil production and consumption, but are also aimed at diversifying supply, gaining greater control over China's foreign oil supplies, and

---

[28]United States Energy Information Administration, "Sudan," www.eia.doe.gov, November 1999.

[29]Hassan Hafidh, "Iraq and China Sign $1.2 Billion Oil Contract," Reuters World Service, 4 June 1997; Winnie Lee, "CNPC's Spree Looks to Fill Supply Gap," *Platt's Oilgram News*, Vol. 75, No. 165, 26 August 1997, p. 1; Baghdad Iraq Television Network, "Oil Contract Signed with China, Officials Comment," 4 June 1997, in *World News Connection (WNC)*, wnc.fedworld.gov (Document ID: 0ebdi6100hgrzq).

[30]United States Energy Information Administration, "Iraq," www.eia.doe.gov, November 1998.

[31]Email correspondence with Chinese oil industry analyst, 8 June 2000.

[32]Fereidun Fesharaki and Kang Wu, *A Survey of Energy Investment Ties Between Asia and the Middle East*, Honolulu, Hawaii: East-West Center, June 1998.

insulating the Chinese economy from price hikes on the international market.

An important goal of China's investments in overseas oil fields is to diversify China's import channels.[33] Diversification of energy sources and markets is a sound strategy for energy security that both the United States and Japan have pursued. According to Gu Shuzhong, director of the Economic Development Research Center of the Chinese Academy of Social Sciences, "Diversity is the foundation of stability in resource supply."[34] The primary objective of the supply diversification strategy is to reduce China's dependence on the Middle East and the sea-lanes stretching from the Persian Gulf to the South China Sea. The Middle East's share of China's imports was 61 percent in 1998[35] and could increase to around 80 percent by 2010.[36] The Chinese government recognizes that the bulk of China's imports will continue to come from the Middle East and is concerned about supply disruptions in this politically volatile region. The establishment of viable alternative sources of supply, such as Central Asia and Russia, could reduce China's vulnerability to embargoes or blockades of Middle Eastern oil supplies.[37]

Some of China's leaders also appear to believe that the purchase of overseas oil fields can improve China's energy security by providing greater control over domestic oil resources. According to one industry analyst, some senior politburo members believe that overseas investment is a better way to ensure that China's energy needs are met than reliance on the market alone. The greater the control Chinese

---

[33]"Kao duoyuanhua baozhang Zhongguo youqi gongying" ("Rely on diversification to guarantee China's oil and gas supply"), *Zhongguo shiyou bao (China Oil News)*, 12 January 2000, p. 1; Li Shulong, "Di san zhi yan kan Zhongguo shiyou" ("The third eye looks at China's oil"), *Zhongguo shiyou bao (China Oil News)*, 18 January 2000, p. 2.

[34]Gu Shuzhong, "PRC Resources Security Assessed," *Zhongguo kexue bao (China Science News)*, 2 December 1998, p. 3, in *WNC* (Document ID: 0f55msm01fsior).

[35]Xu Yihe, "China's Dependence on the Middle East May Increase," *Asian Wall Street Journal*, 30 March 1999, p. 25.

[36]Fereidun Fesharaki and Kang Wu, *Outlook for Energy Demand, Supply, and Government Policies in China*, Honolulu, Hawaii: East-West Center, 29 July 1998.

[37]"Oil Security Risk, Wolf at the Door?" *China Oil, Gas and Petrochemicals*, Vol. 5, No. 10, 15 May 1997, p. 2; "Key Issues of Energy Development Strategy," *Guoji shangbao (International Business Daily)*, 14 July 1998, p. 6, in Foreign Broadcast Information Service (FBIS) (Document ID: FTS19980925001692).

oil companies have over overseas oil, the greater the security of sup-ply.[38] It is unclear, however, how much control China could exercise over its foreign oil concessions during a crisis.

Evidence also suggests that overseas investments are intended to improve China's energy security by protecting it from price fluctuations. According to two Chinese analysts,

> "[U]nless China invests the capital to control some oil resources, any even insignificant international economic, political, or military conflict could affect the supply and demand on the spot market, causing severe interference to our oil imports, to seriously undermine China's economic stability and sustained development."[39]

In 1997, Zhou Yongkang, then president of CNPC, stated that "overseas exploration and development is a better way for China to achieve a stable oil supply because oil price fluctuations make oil imports a high risk."[40] These statements suggest that China is not investing in overseas oil exploration and development projects to profit from hikes in international oil prices but rather to help stabilize the economy during an oil shock. In the event of another oil shock, the Chinese government will be able to pressure state-owned oil companies to forgo windfall profits from higher international oil prices by requiring them to supply Chinese industries at artificially low prices, cushioning the impact of the shock on China's economy.[41]

Despite the intentions of China's energy planners, China's overseas oil investments (see Table 3.1) to date most likely will not enhance China's energy security. CNPC's foreign oil exploration and devel-

---

[38]Rashid and Saywell, p. 48; Philip Andrews-Speed, "China in Petroleum Politics," *Far Eastern Economic Review*, 14 May 1998, p. 37.

[39]Lin Ye and Zhang Zhong, "Models of Development and Trends in Investment for Multinational Oil Companies," *Guoji maoyi (Intertrade)*, 20 August 1997, pp. 29–31, in FBIS (Document ID: FTS19971008000597).

[40]"China Exploring Overseas Petroleum Business," www.chinaeco.com, 8 September 1997.

[41]Wang Yan, president of CNOOC, makes a similar argument. See Zhao Yining and Pu Shurou, "Zhongguo shiyou mianlin de tiaozhan" ("The Challenges Facing China's Oil"), *Liaowang (Outlook)*, No. 9, 3 March 1997, p. 13.

Table 3.1

**Selected Chinese International Oil Exploration and
Development Projects**

Country	Date	Description
Angola	1998	Letter of intent signed for joint construction of a refinery in Lobito City and the purchase of crude oil.
Canada	1992	CNPC Canada purchased reserves for $6.64 million (Canadian).
Canada	1993	CNPC Canada purchased reserves for $5 million (Canadian).
Egypt	1998	The Great Wall Oil Well Drilling Company, a subsidiary of CNPC, and two Egyptian companies signed an agreement to form a joint-investment company; the Chinese side will own a 51 percent share to develop oil and natural gas.
Italy	1997	CNPC formed a joint venture with the Italian oil company Agip to develop oil fields in Central Asia and Africa.
Kazakhstan	1997	CNPC purchased 60 percent of Aktyubinskmunaigaz Production Association for $4.3 billion. CNPC also agreed to assume $71 million of debt, pay $320 million in cash up front, guarantee pensions and housing for approximately 5000 employees, invest in environmental protection measures, and pay royalties to the Kazakh government. Aktyubinskmunaigaz controls three oil fields (Zhanazhol, Kenkiyak One, and Kenkiyak Two) with estimated recoverable reserves of 1 billion barrels.
Kazakhstan	1997	CNPC purchased 51 percent of Uzen field for $1.3 billion plus a promise to conduct a feasibility study on a $3.5 billion oil pipeline to China. Uzen has estimated recoverable reserves of 1.5 billion barrels.
Kuwait	1995	China Petroleum Engineering Construction Company was awarded two construction contracts for $788 million.

Table 3.1—continued

Country	Date	Description
India	1998	CNPC and India's Oil and Natural Gas Corp. ONGC Videsh set up a joint venture to explore for oil in western Kazakhstan, where it has a concession.
Indonesia	1993	China National Offshore Oil Company (CNOOC) purchased a 32.58 percent interest in an oil field in the Straits of Malacca. In 1995, an additional 6.93 percent interest was purchased.
Iraq	1997	A consortium of Chinese oil companies represented by CNPC and North China Industries Corporation signed a 22-year production-sharing contract to develop al-Ahdab field. The consortium's share is 50 percent. The field will be developed for an estimated cost of $1.3 billion after UN sanctions are lifted. It has recoverable reserves of 1.4 billion barrels and a peak production potential of 90,000 b/d.
Mongolia	1998	China's Haufu Industrial Company and Mongolia's Oyuni Undraa Suuba Company signed a $29.7 million contract for oil extraction and the joint construction of a refinery in southeastern Mongolia.
Papua New Guinea	1994	CNPC joined a consortium with other foreign firms, including China International Trust and Investment Corporation, Marubeni, and America Garnet Resource, and won two exploration blocks offshore of Gulf Province in 1994 (Block 160) and 1995 (Block Kamusi).
Nigeria	1997	CNPC began oil exploration in the Chad Basin under an agreement with the Nigerian National Petroleum Company. In 1998, CNPC purchased two blocks—OML 64 and OML 66—in the Niger River delta.
Peru	1993	Sapet Development Corporation, a subsidiary of CNPC, bought the Talara Block for $25 million.

Table 3.1—continued

Country	Date	Description
Sudan	1997	CNPC acquired a 40 percent stake in the Greater Nile Petroleum Operating Company consortium to explore and develop the Heglig and Unity fields, which could hold 8.5 bb to 12.5 bb of oil. A 940-mile pipeline from the fields to the Red Sea was completed in May 1999. CNPC is also assisting with the construction of a 50,000 b/d refinery near Khartoum.
Taiwan	1998	Taiwan's Chinese Petroleum Corp. and CNOOC formally implemented a 1996 contract to explore for oil in the South China Sea.
Thailand	1993	CNPC signed a production-sharing contract to develop Sukhothai field.
Turkmenistan	1998	China Oil and Building Corporation invested $14 million to restore oil wells.
Venezuela	1997	CNPC bought two marginal fields for $359 million. It purchased a field in the Intercampo Norte with a current output of 6700 b/d for $118 million and the Caracoles Block with a current output of 2700 b/d for $241 million.

opment projects are moving slowly and probably will not produce enough oil to offset China's projected growth in oil imports over the next 20 years. Furthermore, transportation and logistical costs may well prevent most of the oil produced in China's overseas oil fields from entering China. This oil will most likely be sold on the international market or swapped for other oil that would enter the Chinese market.[42] In the long run, the best source of energy security for China is likely to be the development of efficient oil markets, although this idea is not yet universally accepted within the Chinese government.[43]

---

[42]I thank Guy Caruso for pointing out that China's foreign oil investments will not greatly enhance China's energy security.

[43]For arguments that markets are the best source of energy security in the long run, see Dennis O'Brien, "Mightier than the Sword: Energy Markets and Global Security," *Harvard International Review*, Vol. 19, No. 3, Summer 1997, pp. 8–11, 62–63; Fereidun Fesharaki, "Oil Markets and Security in Northeast Asia," in Michael Stankiewicz (ed.),

PIPE DREAMS

The Chinese government has also sought to secure and diversify China's energy supply through the construction of pipelines to transport oil from Kazakhstan and Russia to China (see Table 3.2). In 1996, a group of Chinese oil experts called for the construction of a "pan-Asian continental oil bridge" that would consist of a compre-

Table 3.2

Selected Oil Pipeline Projects Involving China

Pipeline	Description	Length	Cost
Kazakhstan-China	This pipeline will stretch from the Uzen field to the Aktyubinsk fields to the Kumkol field in central Kazakhstan to the Xinjiang autonomous region in western China. In September 1997, CNPC signed an agreement to conduct a feasibility study. In August 1999, CNPC shelved this project, citing insufficient production levels.	3000 km	$3.5 billion
Kazakhstan-Iran	This pipeline will head from the Uzen field through Turkmenistan and Iran to the Persian Gulf, from where oil will be shipped to both China and Europe. In September 1997, CNPC signed an agreement to build this pipeline. It appears to be inactive.	1000 km	$1 billion
Russia-China	This pipeline will transport crude from Angarsk in Siberia to China. Two routes are under consideration. One travels to China's northern provinces via Mongolia, while the other travels to China's northeastern provinces, avoiding Mongolia. The Russian oil company has proposed the formation of a consortium for the construction of the pipeline.	2400 km	$2 billion

Energy Security in Northeast Asia: Fueling Security, University of California Institute on Global Conflict and Cooperation, Policy Paper #35, February 1998, pp. 23–25; and Daniel Yergin, Dennis Eklof, and Jefferson Edwards, "Fueling Asia's Recovery," *Foreign Affairs*, Vol. 77, No. 2, March/April 1998, pp. 34–50.

hensive network of pipelines linking suppliers in the Middle East, Central Asia, and Russia to consumers in China and possibly Korea, Japan, and Taiwan. They argued that such a pipeline system would increase both the availability of oil on the world market and oil trade between the countries involved, possibly supplying East Asia with up to 20 percent of its oil needs.[44]

In 1997, CNPC's offer to conduct a feasibility study on the construction of a 3000-km oil pipeline between Kazakhstan and China—part of its bid for development rights to Kazakh oil fields—indicated that part of this "pan-Asian oil bridge" might become a reality. It was estimated to cost $3.5 billion. Most industry analysts, however, dismissed the pipeline as a "pipe dream" because of the high costs its construction would entail. Oil executives familiar with the project suspected that the combined reserves of the Aktyubinsk and Uzen fields were not sufficient to justify it, particularly given that world oil prices had dropped to around US$10 to $12 a year after CNPC agreed to conduct a feasibility study on the pipeline.[45] Some analysts speculated that world oil prices need to be above US$14 to $15 for the pipeline to be economically viable.[46]

The apparent economic infeasibility of the pipeline suggests that the Chinese government's enthusiasm for it stemmed from other reasons. The most valid of these may be concerns on the part of the Chinese government about the security of the country's oil supply.[47] China currently does not possess the naval capabilities necessary to defend its sea shipments of oil and, consequently, regards their passage through waters dominated by the U.S. Navy—especially the Persian Gulf—as a key strategic vulnerability. An overland pipeline

---

[44]"Experts Call for a Pan-Asian Oil Bridge," *Xinhua*, 16 June 1996, in *WNC* (Document ID: 0dt7tt303s348w).

[45]Charles Clover, "Kazakhs and Chinese Press for Oil Deals," *Financial Times*, 6 July 1998, p. 4.

[46]"China's Oil Imports Rise, Possible Boon for U.S.," *Oil & Gas Journal*, 7 June 1999, p. 24.

[47]Indeed, this was one of the main arguments made by Li Peng in favor of CNPC's participation in overseas oil development and production and one of the reasons why he personally assured Kazakhstan's leaders that the Chinese government supported CNPC's investments in Kazakhstan.

that avoids the U.S.-dominated shipping lanes would mitigate China's vulnerability to disruptions of its seaborne oil supplies.

Analysts, both Chinese and Western, have emphasized certain potential strategic advantages of the pipeline. The author of a recent article in *Strategy and Management,* an influential Chinese policy journal, argues that the benefits of an overland pipeline would spill over to the political realm by making China less vulnerable to pressure from the United States and Japan.[48] Xu Xiaojie, who has written extensively but vaguely on the geopolitics of China's energy strategy, argues that China's investment in Kazakhstan would be a means for China to expand its influence there.[49] An example of this was CNPC's request to bring 50,000 workers to Kazakhstan to build the pipeline, which would have created a sizable Chinese presence in the country.[50]

It has also been suggested that the Chinese government hoped that the Kazakhstan-China pipeline would help to foster political stability along its Central Asian border. China's leaders perceive an irredentist threat from Xinjiang's Muslim Uighur population. The Uighurs, who constitute some 46 percent of Xinjiang's population, are culturally and linguistically more similar to their Central Asian neighbors than to their Han Chinese rulers. Uighur separatists in Xinjiang yearn to reestablish their own independent state of East Turkestan, which existed briefly in 1933 and from 1944 until 1950. Ethnic tensions between Uighurs and Han Chinese have been increasing in Xinjiang since the 1980s, with Uighur separatists waging a low-level

---

[48]Zhang Wenmu, "Meiguo de shiyou diyuan zhanlue yu Zhongguo Xizang Xinjiang diqu anquan" ("U.S. Petroleum Geography Strategy and the Security of Tibet and Xinjiang"), *Zhanlue yu guanli (Strategy and Management),* No. 2, 1998, p. 103.

[49]Xu Xiaojie, "The Oil and Gas Linkages Between Central Asia and China: A Geopolitical Perspective," Baker Institute Working Paper, Houston, Texas: Rice University, April 1998; Xu Xiaojie, *Xin shiji de youqi diyuan zhengzhi: Zhongguo mianlin de jiyu yu tiaozhan (The Geopolitics of Oil and Gas in the New Century: The Opportunities and Challenges Facing China),* Beijing: Social Science Literature Press, April 1998.

[50]Charles Clover, "Kazakhs tread softly in the shadow of giant neighbor," *Financial Times,* 3 July 1999, p. 4.

campaign of terror against the Han Chinese.[51] Beijing is determined to prevent the emergence of an independent Uighur state, not only because Xinjiang is rich in natural resources and is an important buffer against the Central Asian frontier, but also because a successful drive for independence in Xinjiang could spark similar movements in Tibet and Taiwan.

The Chinese government has attempted to quash separatist tendencies in the past by promoting the economic enfranchisement of the Uighurs and other minority groups, notably by investments in energy-development projects in Xinjiang.[52] China's leaders had hoped that the pipeline, if constructed, would ease discontent among Xinjiang's Uighur population by creating jobs for them. They also thought that the pipeline would be an added incentive for the Kazakh government to curb the activities of Uighur separatist groups in Kazakhstan.[53]

Despite the potential noneconomic benefits of the pipeline, CNPC, under pressure from the State Council, shelved its construction plans in August 1999 for economic reasons. The Aktyubinsk and Uzen fields do not possess sufficient reserves to justify the pipeline's construction. The projected crude oil production from these fields for the pipeline is estimated to be 152,000 b/d, far below the pipeline design capacity of 500,000 b/d.[54] Furthermore, for the pipeline to be economically viable, the crude would have to cost US$5 per barrel

---

[51]For more information on ethnic tensions in Xinjiang, see James P. Dorian, Brett Wigdortz, and Dru Gladney, "Central Asia and Xinjiang, China: emerging energy, economic, and ethnic relations," *Central Asian Survey*, Vol. 16, No. 4, 1997, pp. 465–467.

[52]Bryan A. Krekel, "Cross-Border Trade and Ethnic Unrest in Xinjiang: Conflict and Cooperation in the Origins of Chinese-Kazakh Energy Relations," unpublished M.A. thesis, University of Washington, 1998, p. 26.

[53]Personal communication with Huaibin Lu of Cambridge Energy Research Associates, 24 June 1998 and 4 February 1999; Rashid and Saywell, p. 48. It should be noted, however, that past efforts on the part of the Chinese government to quell Uighur unrest in Xinjiang through the development of regional energy sources have backfired. Economic benefits from the government's efforts to develop Xinjiang's petroleum industry have largely ended up in the hands of Han Chinese instead of Uighurs, further exacerbating tensions between the two groups. Krekel, p. 26.

[54]"CNPC Shelves China-Kazakhstan Oil Pipeline," *Oil & Gas Journal*, 30 August 1999, p. 44.

less than that purchased from the Middle East, which would have been nearly impossible to accomplish.[55]

With cancellation of the Kazakhstan-China pipeline, China will not have a significant source of overland oil imports from Central Asia. Rail transport of Kazakh oil to China is not a viable option in the long term. Crude production in Xinjiang already exceeds the province's refining capacity, necessitating that surplus crude be transported eastward by railway. However, the two Xinjiang-to-Lanzhou rail lines are near full capacity and eventually will be unable to handle extra crude oil from either Xinjiang or Kazakhstan. This situation is further complicated by the fact that the projected surplus volume of crude is unlikely to justify the cost of either a third rail line or a long-distance oil pipeline.[56] As a result, the oil that CNPC produces in Kazakhstan will most likely be swapped with refiners located near the Uzen and Aktyubinsk fields. CNPC has already signed a swap agreement with Russia's Yukos.[57] If a pipeline is built from Neka, an oil port on the southern shore of the Caspian, to Tehran, then CNPC could provide crude to refiners in northern Iran in return for an equal amount exported from the Persian Gulf to China.[58]

The Chinese government's efforts to construct the Russia-China segment of the "pan-Asian continental oil bridge" appear to be more promising, in contrast with its experience with the Kazakhstan-China oil pipeline. Officials from both countries are discussing the construction of an oil pipeline from Angarsk in Siberia to China. Two routes are under consideration. One would travel to the northern provinces of China via Mongolia, while the other would travel to the

---

[55]Quan Lan, "Transnational oil pipeline shelved," *China Oil, Gas and Petrochemicals*, Vol. 7, No. 16, 15 August 1999, pp. 2–3.

[56]Not-for-attribution report prepared by an international consulting firm for the KazTrans Oil Company.

[57]"Russia to Increase Oil Supplies to China," *Moscow Interfax*, 7 September 1999, in *WNC* (Document ID: 0fhssxc041212p).

[58]The National Iranian Oil Company (NIOC) snubbed a bid for the construction of this pipeline by CNPC and Sinopec in 1999. NIOC sent a delegation to Beijing in January 2000 to ask the companies to reconsider, but the companies' enthusiasm for the project appears to have waned, probably as a result of pressure from the State Council facing doubts about the pipeline's economic feasibility. "Tehran Presses Beijing on Neka-Tehran Bid," *Hart's Asian Petroleum News*, Vol. 4, No. 4, 31 January 2000.

northeastern provinces of China, avoiding Mongolia. Russia's Ministry of Fuel and Energy is in favor of the first route because it is 170 km shorter, whereas Chinese officials prefer the second route because the political risk is lower. The pipeline, estimated to cost US$2 billion, is expected to transport around 220 million barrels of oil per year. Industry sources indicate that an agreement for the construction of this pipeline will be signed during the Sino-Russian summit in June 2000, with a feasibility study to begin immediately afterward.[59]

PLANS FOR A STRATEGIC PETROLEUM RESERVE

Concerns about energy security have prompted the Chinese government to seriously consider the construction of a strategic petroleum reserve (SPR), perhaps with help from the International Energy Agency (IEA).[60] The IEA regards the maintenance of strategic reserves as a key measure oil-importing countries can take to increase their ability to manage changes in the international oil market. Chinese advocates of the establishment of an SPR contend that it could enhance China's energy security in several ways.

First, construction of an SPR would reduce China's vulnerability to short-term oil-supply interruptions. Chinese analysts recognize that China's growing dependence on Middle Eastern oil imports means that its vulnerability to disruptions of its oil supply from this potentially unstable region will also increase. There have been 13 significant disruptions of Middle Eastern crude oil supplies since 1951, and the possibility of future supply interruptions, however remote, still exists.[61] There is also concern in China that the flow of oil between the Middle East and China could be impeded by transportation acci-

---

[59]"Yukos to Organize Consortium for Construction of Oil Pipeline to China," *Russian Oil and Gas Report*, 31 March 2000; Sergei Blagov, "Russian Firms Resolve Siberia-PRC Oil Pipeline Dispute," *South China Morning Post*, 9 February 2000, p. 3.

[60]Fesharaki and Wu, "Outlook for Energy Demand, Supply, and Government Policies in China," p. 32.

[61]Zhao Hongtu and Li Rong, "Jianli woguo zhanlue shiyou chubei shizai bixing" ("Need for China to Establish Strategic Petroleum Reserves"), *Guoji shiyou jingji (International Petroleum Economics)*, Vol. 7, No. 2, March 1999, p. 26; Ma Hong and Sun Zhu, "Jianli woguo zhanlue shiyou chubei de zhengzhi kaolü" ("Thoughts on Establishing China's Strategic Petroleum Reserve"), *Zhanlue yu guanli (Strategy and Management)*, No. 1, 1997, p. 47; and "Oil Security Risk, Wolf at Door?" p. 2.

dents because of the growing number of oil tankers passing through the Straits of Malacca.

Second, an SPR could help stabilize domestic prices in the event of dramatic oil increases on the international market. The Chinese government is extremely concerned about how China would weather oil shocks similar to those of the 1970s. China was a net oil exporter at that time and followed OPEC's lead in increasing the price of its exports. Now that China is a net oil importer, however, it is vulnerable to sudden market changes.[62]

Third, an SPR could deter politically or economically motivated supply disruptions. Some Chinese analysts point out that strategic reserves could make oil-producing countries think twice about imposing an embargo. The ability to draw on strategic reserves could similarly deter third countries from implementing an oil blockade against oil shipments to China.[63]

Fourth, two analysts further argue that an SPR could increase China's diplomatic room to maneuver. Shielded from the adverse effects of a short-term supply disruption, China could take actions that, lacking strategic reserves, it presumably would not pursue. The analysts do not specify what these activities might be, however, instead arguing that if self-sufficient, China could assist other countries, increase its influence, and raise its international position.[64]

An SPR would improve China's energy security, reducing its vulnerability to supply disruptions and presumably easing Chinese concerns about a growing reliance on oil imports, in general, and Middle Eastern oil imports, in particular. Oil import dependency does not equal vulnerability if an alternative supply exists. Thus, China could be 100 percent dependent on oil imports but be relatively invulnerable to oil supply disruptions if it possessed large

---

[62]Zhao Hongtu and Li Rong, p. 26; Ma Hong and Sun Zhu, p. 47; "A Slump in Oil Prices Badly Hits China," *Jingji ribao (Economic Daily)*, 21 May 1998, p. 7, in *WNC* (Document ID: 0evdnoa03486k); Chang Weimin, "Legislation Needed for Oil Reserve," *China Daily Business Weekly*, 8 June 1997, p. 1.

[63]Zhao Hongtu and Li Rong, p. 26; Ma Hong and Sun Zhu, p. 47.

[64]Zhao Hongtu and Li Rong, p. 26.

reserves.[65]   However, construction and operation costs are a major impediment to the realization of China's plans to establish an SPR; these costs are estimated to be around US$5 per barrel for a salt cavern facility with a unit capacity of 100 million barrels.[66]

REFINERY EXPANSION TO PROCESS MIDDLE EASTERN CRUDES

China also seeks to enhance its energy security through the expansion of its refining capacity with facilities capable of processing Middle Eastern crudes. Construction of such facilities is necessitated not only by China's growing reliance on oil imports from the Middle East but also by the recent decision of China's energy planners to meet the country's oil needs by processing crude imports instead of importing refined products.[67]   This strategy reflects the Chinese government's opinion that crude imports are a better source of energy security than refined imports,[68] perhaps because refined products are more expensive to store and deteriorate more quickly than crude oil.

Most of China's existing refineries are unable to process Middle Eastern crudes, which have a higher sulfur content than current sources. China competes with Japan, South Korea, and other large importers for the low-sulfur crudes produced in Asia, and China's energy planners are aware that the export availability is in decline. Consequently, China will become increasingly reliant on the Middle East for crude supplies. The share of total crude imports provided by the Middle East is projected to increase from 48 percent in 1997 to 81 percent in 2010 (see Figure 3.1).[69] Oman is currently China's largest

---

[65]Guy Caruso, in comments on an earlier version of this report, 8 October 1999.

[66]*Emergency Oil Stocks and Energy Security in the APEC Region*, Tokyo, Japan: Asia Pacific Energy Research Centre, March 2000, p. 53, www.ieej.or.jp/aperc/REPORTS.html, citing PB-KBB Inc., *Strategic Oil Storage Concepts and Costs for Asia Pacific Region*, Final Draft Report, prepared for Asia Pacific Energy Research Centre, 30 October 1998.

[67]"China to Import Crude, Not Products: Energy Security Analysis," *Asia Pulse*, 20 January 2000.

[68]Fesharaki and Wu, *Outlook for Energy Demand, Supply, and Government Policies in China*, p. 22.

[69]Fesharaki and Wu, pp. 14, 19.

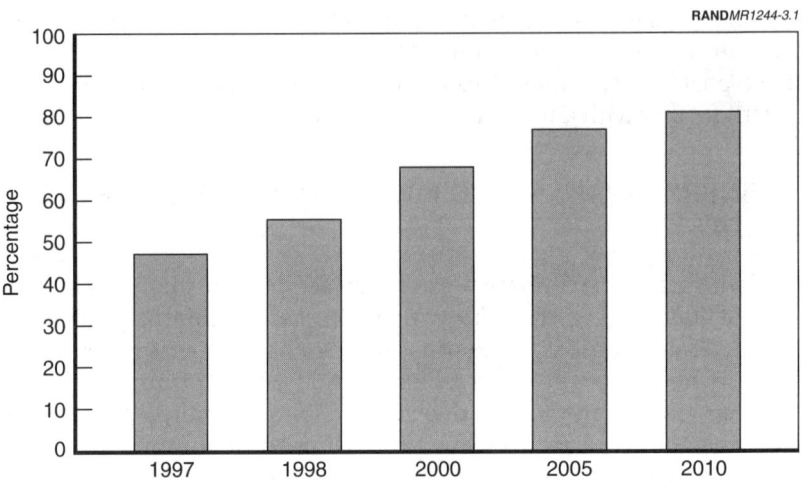

SOURCE: Fereidun Fesharaki and Kang Wu, *Outlook for Energy Demand, Supply, and Government Policies in China*, Honolulu, Hawaii: East-West Center, 29 July 1998.

Figure 3.1—Share of Middle Eastern Crude Oil in China's Total Crude Imports

supplier of crude oil, followed by Yemen, Indonesia, and Iran. Saudi Arabia's share of China's crude imports is projected to grow (see Table 3.3).[70] China's refineries can refine "sweet" (low in sulfur content) crudes from Oman and Yemen but not the "sour" (high in sulfur content) crudes from countries such as Iran, Iraq, Saudi Arabia, and Kuwait.

The upgrading and expansion of China's coastal refineries is thus a top priority for both the Chinese government and Middle Eastern oil companies eager to break into China's domestic market. The Chinese government hopes to establish long-term energy ties with

---

[70]Chen Wenxian, "Jiang likely to bring home more crude from Saudi Arabia," *China Oil, Gas and Petrochemicals*, Vol. 7, No. 21, 1 November 1999, pp. 9–10, 13.

Table 3.3

China's Top Sources of Crude Imports in 1999

Country	Share of Total Imports (%)
Oman	13.7
Yemen	11.3
Indonesia	10.8
Iran	10.8
Angola	7.9
Saudi Arabia	6.8
United Kingdom	6.0
Norway	5.5
Vietnam	4.1
Angola	3.7

SOURCE: Fan Wenxin, "China's oil trade hits record highs in 1999," *China Oil, Gas and Petrochemicals*, Vol. 8, No. 3, 1 February 2000, p. 13.

oil-producing countries in the Middle East[71] and has devoted considerable effort to attracting foreign investment from Saudi Arabia, Kuwait, and Iran for refining joint ventures that could secure a large portion of the oil that China needs. This strategy dovetails with the exporting countries' long-term plans to find secure markets for their oil. Saudi Aramco, which has been working for years to establish a presence in China, has a 25 percent stake in a refinery expansion project in Fujian Province. The company is awaiting government approval of its proposal to build a refinery in Shandong Province with Ssangyong of Korea and Sinochem of China. In November 1999, Saudi Arabia and China signed an agreement to build a 240,000 b/d refinery in Fujian Province that will use oil from Saudi Arabia.[72] The Kuwait Petroleum Corporation (KPC) has a 14.3 percent stake in China's offshore Yacheng 13-1 gas field. KPC officials are negotiating with CNPC for participation in the expansion of the Qilu refinery. If

---

[71] This perspective is reflected in Shen Qinyu and Wu Lei, "Focus on the Gulf Region in Developing Oil Industry," *Guoji maoyi wenti (International Trade Journal)*, No. 2, 6 February 1995, pp. 9–12, in *WNC* (Document ID: 0dils8r002sg6p); Ma Xiuqing, "Zhongguo de shiyou jinkou xuyao he tong Alabo guojia shiyou hezuo de fazhan" ("China's Demand for Oil Imports and the Development of Its Cooperation with Arab Oil-Producing States"), *Xiya Feizhou (West Asia and Africa)*, No. 2, 1997, pp. 16–21.

[72] "PRC, Saudi Arabia to Build Refinery in Fujian," *Wen wei po*, 3 November 1999, p. A2; in FBIS (Document ID: FTS19991103000187).

successful, KPC would receive an equity share in exchange for a long-term supply contract. Iran has also promised to provide funds to upgrade a refinery in the south that will enable it to process medium-sulfur Iranian crudes, but no firm deal has been signed.[73]

DEVELOPMENT OF THE NATURAL GAS INDUSTRY

The Chinese government can also improve China's energy security through development of the country's natural gas industry. Greater use of natural gas in China has been hindered by the absence of a bureaucratic champion for gas, the remote location of China's gas reserves, an inadequate pipeline infrastructure, lack of a well-developed market, and insufficient funding. However, over the past few years, the Chinese government has expanded the role of natural gas in China's energy structure, primarily as a result of concern over China's growing dependency on oil imports and widespread environmental degradation caused by coal. Other reasons for the high priority placed on natural gas development include chronic energy shortages and imbalances, increasingly competitive prices for natural gas vis-à-vis coal, and greater competition among China's state-owned oil companies for shares of the natural gas market—a result of industrial reform. Fertilizer and chemical plants currently consume most of China's natural gas, but the government has targeted the urban industrial and residential sectors and the transportation sector for greater natural gas use.[74]

The Chinese government has stepped up its efforts to develop domestic gas reserves. The participation of foreign oil companies in gas development projects is encouraged because of the technological and financial constraints faced by China's oil companies and the government's desire to bring reserves on line as quickly as possible. CNPC and Shell recently signed a letter of intent to develop the Changbei natural gas field at the border of northern China's Shaanxi Province and the Inner Mongolia autonomous region. It is projected that after this US$3 billion project is completed in 2004, it will annu-

---

[73]Fesharaki and Wu, *A Survey of Energy Investment Ties Between Asia and the Middle East*, pp. 21–22.

[74]Jeffrey Logan and William Chandler, "Natural Gas Gains Momentum," *China Business Review*, Vol. 25, No. 4, July-August 1998, pp. 40–45.

ally supply 105.9 tcf of gas to eastern China within 20 years.[75] The Chinese government has also approved a proposed natural gas pipeline from the Xinjiang autonomous region to Shanghai municipality. Construction is expected to begin in 2001 at an estimated cost of US$7.23 billion for the pipeline alone and an additional US$6 billion for gas exploration in Xinjiang. CNPC plans to be the dominant shareholder. Foreign participation in the project is welcome. However, according to a Chinese official, foreign investors will not be granted access to the project's operations because of energy security concerns—possibly a fear of foreign control over China's gas resources.[76]

The Chinese government plans to supplement China's limited natural gas reserves with both liquefied natural gas (LNG) and pipeline imports. In January 2000, the government approved plans for the construction of an LNG terminal in Shenzhen, Guangdong Province. Industry reports indicate that domestic investors will have a 65 percent stake in the project, with CNOOC as the majority shareholder. The remaining 35 percent will be offered to foreign investors. The project is estimated to cost US$3.68 billion. The first phase of construction will provide an LNG to Guangzhou, Shenzhen, Foshan, and Dongguan and will be completed in 2005. The second phase will expand coverage to five other cities by 2010.[77] Guangdong constitutes a large potential market for LNG because it is located so far from China's coal-producing regions that LNG imports are likely to be less expensive than domestically produced coal. There are also plans for a second LNG terminal to be built near Shanghai.

Chinese energy planners are also seriously considering importing natural gas through pipelines (see Table 3.4). The construction of a pipeline from the Kovyktinskoye field near Irkutsk in eastern Siberia through Mongolia to northeastern China and possibly South Korea and Japan has been the subject of negotiation between China and

---

[75]"China's CNPC and Shell to Co-Develop Natural Gas Field," *Asia Pulse*, 20 March 2000.

[76]Gong Zhengzheng, "Xinjiang Gas Heading to Shanghai," *China Daily Business Weekly*, 30 January 2000, p. 1.

[77]"China's Guangdong Invites Bids for Liquefied Gas Project," *Asia Pulse*, 14 February 2000.

Table 3.4

Selected Natural Gas Pipeline Projects Involving China

Pipeline	Description	Length	Cost
Xinjiang-Shanghai	This pipeline will transport natural gas from northwestern China to consumers in eastern China. CNPC will be the dominant shareholder. BP-Amoco and Enron are interested in this project.	4200 km	$7.25 billion
Turkmenistan-China-Korea-Japan	The natural gas pipeline will run from Turkmenistan via Uzbekistan and Kazakhstan to Lianyungang in China's Jiangsu Province with possible extensions to Korea and Japan. CNPC, Exxon, and Mitsubishi recently completed a feasibility study.	6250 km to China, 8500 km with extensions to Korea and Japan	$9.5 billion to China, $22 billion with extensions to Korea and Japan
Russia-China	The natural gas pipeline will run from Kovyktinskoye field near Irkutsk in eastern Siberia to either Beijing or the port of Rizhao in Shandong Province via Mongolia. In February 1999, Russia and China signed an agreement to complete a feasibility study on this line. South Korea is interested in the project.	2500 km to Beijing, 3400 km to Rizhao	$8–$12 billion

Russia for many years. The first official expression of the two countries' intent to develop this pipeline was a memorandum of understanding signed between CNPC and the Russian Ministry of Fuel and Energy in November 1994.[78] Both sides signed agreements on the construction of the pipeline during Russian Prime Minister Viktor Chernomyrdin's visit to Beijing in June 1997 and during the Sino-

---

[78]Quan Lan and Keun-Wook Paik, *China Natural Gas Report*, London: Royal Institute of International Affairs, 1998, p. 106.

Soviet summit meeting in November 1997. The June accord envisioned the export of approximately 2 billion cubic feet per day (bcf/d) for 30 years. The November accord indicated that of the approximately 2 bcf/d the pipeline is expected to carry, 1 bcf/d would go to China and the remainder would be available to South Korea and Japan. It also proposed that the pipeline be completed in 30 months at a cost of US$12 billion. Neither accord specified how the pipeline would be financed.[79] In February 1999, China and Russia signed a deal to conduct a feasibility study on the pipeline, which is expected to take up to three years to complete.[80]

Progress on the Irkutsk pipeline project has been slowed because the northern China gas market—the proposed destination for Kovyktinskoye gas—is currently unable to support the proposed pipeline. The amount of natural gas that the pipeline is expected to supply to northern China—1 billion bcf/d—is triple the amount of gas consumed in the region today. For the market to expand, it needs immediate large consumers (power generators, factories converting their boilers to gas, fertilizer plants) for the gas supplied by the pipeline. However, there is not much demand for gas-fueled power generators today because China has an oversupply of power and coal is often a cheaper fuel than gas. Demand for boiler conversion is limited because it is expensive and many boilers are located in money-losing state-owned enterprises. Furthermore, there is not now an acute need for new fertilizer. Industry experts predict that it will be at least a decade before the northern China market can absorb the 1 bcf/d the Irkutsk pipeline is expected to deliver.[81]

Another reason for the inertia of the Irkutsk pipeline project is that how the pipeline will be funded has not been resolved. Estimates of the cost of the pipeline range from US$8 billion to US$12 billion, depending on the proposed length, diameter, and the number of compressor stations.[82] China and Russia cannot finance the pipeline

---

[79]Christoffersen, pp. 22–23; Steve Liesman, "Russia-to-China Natural Gas Pipeline Is Agreed Upon at Yeltsin-Jiang Summit," *Wall Street Journal*, 11 November 1997, p. A14.

[80]Sergei Blagov, "Russia-Asia: Hard Times Aside, Moscow Still Eyes Gas Supply," *Interpress Service*, 31 May 1999.

[81]Interview with Scott Roberts of Cambridge Energy Research Associates, Beijing, China, 23 March 2000.

[82]Quan and Paik, pp. 108–109.

alone. Both countries initially expected that Japan and South Korea would invest in the pipelines; South Korea, for example, has a huge potential natural gas market. The country pays a premium for LNG imports and may view Kovyktinskoye gas as a cheaper alternative. Japan is also a large consumer of natural gas, and concerns about acid rain may be a factor in Japanese interest. The Japanese government has invested in a number of clean energy projects in China and may view the Irkutsk pipeline as another way to reduce China's use of coal and the damage it does to Japan's environment. Although the Asian financial situation casts doubts on Japan's and South Korea's participation in the pipeline project, media reports indicate that the South Korean state-run company Kogas is still interested.[83]

Another transnational gas pipeline that may become economically viable as China's gas market develops is the proposed line between Turkmenistan and the coastal city of Lianyungang in China's Jiangsu Province, with a possible extension to Japan via South Korea. CNPC and Mitsubishi proposed, to Turkmenistan's president in 1992, exporting Turkmen gas to China. During Li Peng's visit to Turkmenistan in 1994, CNPC and the Turkmenistan Ministry of Oil and Gas signed a letter of intent to establish a commission to study the pipeline. One year later, CNPC, Mitsubishi, and Exxon agreed to conduct a feasibility study, which they reportedly completed in 1996.[84] The length of the pipeline (6200 km onshore and 2300 km offshore) and the limited gas market in China make this pipeline a highly risky project to undertake today. However, once the pipeline between Xinjiang and Shanghai is constructed, the Turkmenistan project will become more economically feasible because the gas from Turkmenistan can flow through the Xinjiang-Shanghai pipeline.

Chinese writings generally regard the development of China's natural gas industry and the import of natural gas as ways to improve China's energy security. Not only would natural gas imports enable China to diversify its energy supply sources (provided they do not

---

[83] "Kogas to Take Part in Gas Pipeline Construction Project Linking Kovyktinskoye Gas Field to China," *Russian Oil and Gas Report*, 11 October 1999.

[84] Quan and Paik, pp. 112–113, Christoffersen, p. 25.

originate in the Middle East), but they could also help lessen China's dependence on foreign oil and vulnerability to oil supply disruptions.[85] Gas imports supplied by a pipeline traveling through Chinese territory would also provide China's planners with a degree of psychological security,[86] although this has not been explicitly mentioned in Chinese writings.

Chinese analysts realize, however, that natural gas security could become an issue. Pipeline imports, although generally perceived in China as being more secure than tanker imports, cannot guarantee absolute energy security; supply disruptions are still possible.[87] LNG imports, particularly from the Middle East, would be as vulnerable as oil imports to embargoes, blockades, and transportation accidents. Furthermore, some senior leaders and commanders of the People's Liberation Army reportedly regard the construction of a natural gas pipeline from Russia as a threat to China's energy and national security on the grounds that it would make China unnecessarily vulnerable to supply cutoffs during a regional or global crisis.[88]

OPENING THE DOOR TO OIL

The central government's desire to reduce China's reliance on oil imports by exploiting untapped domestic reserves has prompted the gradual opening of onshore drilling areas to foreign participation, notably in the Tarim Basin in the northwestern autonomous region

---

[85]"PRC Sees Natural Gas as Supplement to Petroleum," *Xinhua,* 16 October 1997, in *WNC* (Document ID: 0eih70r03suv37); Yang Qing, "Yao cong zhanlue gaodu zhongshi LNG jinkou" ("Pay Attention to LNG Imports in High-Level Strategy"), *Zhongguo nengyuan (Energy of China)*, No. 5, 1998, p. 5.

[86]Quan and Paik, p. 116.

[87]Ji Guoxing, "Yatai nengyuan anquan hezuo: xingshi yu renwu" ("Energy Security Cooperation in the Asia-Pacific Region: Situation and Mission"), *Guoji guancha (International Survey)*, No. 3, 1999, p. 10; Yan Xuetong, "Zhongguo fazhan miandui de guoji anquan huanjing" ("The International Security Environment Facing China's Development"), in *Guoji xingshi fenxi baogao (Study Reports on the International Situation)*, Beijing: China Society for Strategy and Management Research, 1998, p. 8; and Yang Qing, p. 7.

[88]Malcolm Nixon, "BP-Amoco—Wrong Footed Again?" *Hart's Asian Petroleum News*, Vol. 3, No. 43, 1 November 1999; and Mehmet Ögütçü, "China's Energy Future and Global Implications," in Werner Draguhn and Robert Ash (eds.), *China's Economic Security*, New York: St. Martin's Press, 1999, p. 137.

of Xinjiang. Foreign involvement is regarded as a means of improving China's energy security because multinational oil companies possess the technology, capital, and managerial skills necessary to maximize China's onshore production. The Chinese government hopes that cooperation with foreign companies will enable China to develop a world-class oil industry.

Foreign companies have been active in China's petroleum sector since 1982. The Chinese government initially limited foreign participation to offshore areas to gain expertise without surrendering control over China's major onshore production bases. Offshore exploration, however, has been a great disappointment. In 1996, it produced only some 73.3 million barrels, a mere 10 percent of domestic production at a cost two to three times higher than that of onshore wells. Consequently, both Chinese officials and foreign contractors now realize that any hope for a domestic solution to China's oil insufficiency lies onshore in the Tarim Basin.[89]

Foreign companies have been permitted to conduct onshore exploration since 1985, but the Chinese government did not open the Tarim Basin to foreigners until almost a decade later. In 1993, the government invited foreign companies to bid for five blocks in the southeastern part of the Tarim Basin, largely out of recognition that China did not possess the funds, technology, or management skills necessary to develop such a large and difficult field.[90]

Concerns about self-sufficiency appear to have colored the debate about foreign participation in China's onshore petroleum industry. China's top leaders were divided over whether inland areas should be open to foreign companies.[91] CNPC was similarly internally split

---

[89]Becquelin, p. 24.

[90]The Tarim Basin is a Texas-sized area with complex geological structures and surface conditions that are arguably more difficult than those of any other onshore basin. More than half of the basin is covered by the Taklimakan desert, which has no oases in its interior and sand finer than that of the Arabian peninsula, making the movement and operation of machinery arduous. Oil is found as deep as 6000 meters, making drilling expensive and technically challenging. Surface temperatures are extremely cold in the winter and hot in the summer. Robert Tansey, "Black Gold Rush," *China Business Review*, Vol. 21, No. 4, July-August 1994, p. 14.

[91]Becquelin, p. 24.

over how much foreign participation to allow.[92] First, the company was reluctant to give jobs to foreign companies when it had 1.4 million workers on its payroll, some of whom could be transferred from the declining fields in the east to the Tarim Basin. Second, company officials hoped to enhance their careers with a major discovery in the Tarim Basin. Many of the company's top officials had achieved their positions from association with major discoveries at Daqing field and hoped to repeat their success out west. Junior officials hoped for similar career-enhancing discoveries.[93] The company's Tarim office was particularly opposed to the central government's decision to open the basin to foreign companies. Their opposition may have influenced the decision to offer marginal blocks to foreign companies, while reserving the most promising ones for CNPC.[94] The dry wells drilled by foreign companies and the failure of CNPC to make a major discovery in choice blocks dampened foreign interest in Tarim, despite the offering of eight additional blocks in 1995.

Recent developments suggest that the recognition by many Chinese officials that foreign participation in onshore oil exploration and development projects is crucial to reducing China's reliance on imported oil could result in greater foreign involvement in China's oil sector. In a major policy statement published in the Communist Party journal *Seeking Truth* in 1997, then-Premier Li Peng stressed the importance of using both foreign and domestic capital to develop China's resources.[95] The newly revised *Guiding Catalogue for Foreign Investment in Industry* officially encourages foreign involvement in certain petroleum, petrochemical, and chemical projects such as technology for tertiary oil recovery and oil pipeline and depot construction and management.[96] Furthermore, new regions are now open to foreign companies, mainly in western China and the

---

[92]Yatsko, p. 69.

[93]Julia Leung, "China Takes Risk in Policy on Oil Basins," *Asian Wall Street Journal*, 27 May 1991, cited in Keun-Wook Paik, *Gas and Oil in Northeast Asia: Policies, Projects, and Prospects*, London: Royal Institute of International Affairs, 1995, pp. 168–169.

[94]Becquelin, p. 24.

[95]Li Peng, "China's Policy on Energy Resources," *Xinhua*, 28 May 1997, in *WNC* (Document ID: drchi119-n-97001).

[96]David Blumenthal and Gray Sasser, "Fuel for the Next Century," *China Business Review*, Vol. 25, No. 4, July-August 1998, pp. 34–38.

Songliao Plain, for risky exploration and development.   Japan
National Oil Corporation became the first foreign interest to gain access to some of the better blocks in the Tarim Basin in 1997. CNPC
had 27 foreign contracts under execution in 1999.[97]

---

[97]Quan Lan, "Sino-foreign onshore cooperation after IPO," *China Oil, Gas and Petrochemicals*, Vol. 8, No. 8, 15 April 2000, p. 3.

Chapter Four

IMPLICATIONS OF CHINA'S ENERGY
SECURITY ACTIVITIES

Right – but they also fundamentally have a need for a larger energy supply than they can domestically provide. Is it just fear over foreign dependence or is it also recognizing that they need to provide now?

The Chinese government's fear of dependence on foreign oil lies behind its energy security activities. The government's unease with its status as a net oil importer has its origins in China's unhappy experience with Soviet participation in China's oil sector in the 1950s and China's use of its oil exports to Japan to influence Japanese foreign policy in the 1970s. As mentioned earlier, Soviet advisers had a major impact on the development of China's oil industry in the 1950s. Their departure following the Sino-Soviet split in 1960 created severe energy shortages and left China dependent on the Soviet Union, its new adversary, for more than 50 percent of its critical refined oil products. After China became an oil exporter in the 1970s, the Chinese government emulated the Soviet Union in its use of oil exports as a foreign policy tool. China sold oil to Japan at below-market prices in order to dampen Japanese enthusiasm for investment in Siberian oil and gas development projects. The Chinese leadership was afraid that the development of these resources would strengthen the transportation and communications infrastructure in Siberia and enhance the Soviet Union's ability to attack northeastern China, the country's industrial heartland and region of greatest strategic vulnerability.[1] These experiences made

---

[1] For more information on China's use of its oil exports as a political tool, see Choon-ho Park and Jerome Alan Cohen, "The Politics of the Oil Weapon," *Foreign Policy*, No. 20, Fall 1975, pp. 28–40; Woodward, pp. 49–66 and 122–127; and Ronald C. Keith, China's 'Resource Diplomacy' and National Energy Policy," in Ronald C. Keith (ed.), *Energy Security and Economic Development in East Asia*, London: Croom Helm, 1986, pp. 17–78.

China's leaders acutely aware that dependence on foreign oil can bring foreign economic and political pressures that can threaten national security. The Chinese government's fears of foreign oil dependency and the possible exploitation of this vulnerability have resurfaced now that China is once again a net oil importer.[2]

Chinese analysts view the United States as a major threat to China's energy security. The United States is the most powerful country in the world in military, economic, and technological terms. Many Chinese analysts perceive the United States to be uncomfortable with China's rising power and are suspicious that the United States seeks to constrain China's emergence as a potential rival. They cite as evidence American criticism of China's human rights record, arms sales to Taiwan, the deployment of two aircraft carrier battle groups to the waters around Taiwan during China's 1996 missile tests, the revision of the U.S.-Japan security guidelines, the bombing of the Chinese Embassy in Belgrade, the passage of the Taiwan Security Enhancement Act by the United States House of Representatives, and the possible deployment of Theater Missile Defense (TMD) and National Missile Defense (NMD) systems.[3] Of particular concern to Chinese analysts is that there is no state (or groups of states) powerful enough to balance against the United States. They regard China as being especially vulnerable to American power in a world in which the United States is the sole superpower.[4]

---

[2]These fears are explicitly addressed in "Article Examines 21st Century Oil Strategy," *Liaowang (Outlook)*, No. 9, 3 March 1997, pp. 14–16, in James Mulvenon (ed.), *China Facts and Figures Handbook*, Vol. 21, Gulf Breeze, FL: Academic International Press, 1997, pp. 272–276; "Energy: The New Oil Frontier"; and Shen Qinyu and Wu Lei.

[3]See, for example, Yan Xuetong, "China's Strategic Security Environment," *Shijie zhishi (World Affairs)*, No. 3, February 2000, pp. 8–10, in FBIS (Document ID: FTS2000021600038); Yan Xuetong, "The International Security Environment that China's Development Faces," pp. 6–7; Liu Jiangyong, "Xin 'RiMei fangwei hezuo zhizhen' yu ZhongRi guanxi" ("New 'Guidelines for Japanese-U.S. Cooperative Defense' and Sino-Japanese Relations"), in *Guoji xingshi fenxi baogao (Study Reports on the International Situation)*, Beijing: China Society for Strategy and Management Research, 1998, p. 19; and Huang Hong and Ji Ming, "United under the Great Banner of Patriotism—Thoughts on Strong Condemnations against U.S.-led Atrocities," *Renmin ribao (People's Daily)*, 27 May 1999, p. 9, in FBIS (Document ID: FTS19990603002066).

[4]See, for example, Xiao Feng, "Views on Some Hot-Spot Issues in International Situation," *Xiandai guoji guanxi (Contemporary International Relations)*, No. 12, December 1999, pp. 1–5, in FBIS (Document ID: FTS20000212000168); and Chu

China's recent shift from a net oil exporter to a net oil importer means that energy security is another issue the United States could exploit to pressure China. The Chinese government is uncomfortable with the fact that the United States Navy dominates the sea-lanes stretching from the Persian Gulf to the South China Sea through which the bulk of China's oil imports must pass. There is a concern that if Sino-U.S. relations sour, the United States could use its superior military power to disrupt China's oil supply. Indeed, an article in the Chinese international affairs journal *World Economics and Politics* contends that the United States could use its control of Middle East oil to "check" China.[5] Another Chinese commentary goes even further and argues that the United States has already implemented an "energy containment" policy against China. This policy's objective, according to the article, is to weaken China by gaining control of the energy resources in western China and blocking China's access to oil imports.[6] The United States currently is not pursuing such a policy, but Chinese analysts clearly consider the interruption of its oil supply as a possible future containment measure.

Although not explicitly mentioned by Chinese analysts, it is also possible that the United States could apply oil sanctions against China to punish behavior it deems undesirable on a variety of issues ranging from human rights abuses to arms sales. Economic sanctions have been an important tool of U.S. foreign policy in the post–Cold War era. Given China's vulnerability to U.S. economic pressure and relative lack of allies, the threat and imposition of oil sanctions could appeal to the United States.

China's energy security activities are aimed, in part, to reduce the vulnerability of China's oil supply to American power. China's interest and investment in the development of Central Asian and Russian energy resources can largely be explained by the Chinese perception

---

Shulong, "Sino-US Relations: The Necessity for Change and a New Strategy," *Contemporary International Relations*, Vol. 6, No. 11, November 1996, p. 8.

[5]Wu Lei, "Zhongdong shiyou yu woguo weilai shiyou gongqiu pingheng" ("Middle East Oil and Our Equilibrium of Oil Supply and Demand in the Future"), *Shijie jingji yu zhengzhi (World Economics and Politics)*, No. 3, 1997, pp. 30–33.

[6]Sun Tan, "Mei dui Hua 'nengyuan ezhi' bu neng decheng" ("America's 'Energy Containment Policy' Against China Will Not Succeed"), *Zhongguo kuangye bao (China Mining News)*, 15 December 1999, p. 3.

that these regions are less vulnerable to U.S. power than is the Persian Gulf and the sea-lanes connecting it to the South China Sea. Meanwhile, China's "oil diplomacy" in the Middle East is an effort to ensure continued access to oil from a U.S.-dominated region that provides China with the bulk of its oil imports. These activities reflect Beijing's larger strategy of attempting to reduce its vulnerability to American power through the development of a broad network of secure bilateral relationships, particularly with its neighbors.[7] Similarly, the internationalization of CNPC is a way for China to gain a foothold in the world oil market, which is dominated by companies from the United States, Japan, and Europe. Finally, the Chinese government is pursuing a number of other measures to reduce the amount of oil it has to import and to increase China's ability to manage supply disruptions, including those created by the United States.

Chinese analysts regard Central Asia as a region where energy exports to China are less vulnerable to American power. A report on Central Asia published by the China Society for Strategy and Management Research, a Beijing-based research institute, argues that U.S. involvement in Central Asia does not directly threaten China's energy security. Although the United States is a competitor for Central Asian energy resources, its ability to threaten China's oil supply from this region is limited. Not only did CNPC defeat several major American oil companies in acquiring development rights to Kazakhstan's Uzen and Aktyubinsk oil fields, but geography dictates that Central Asia's energy cooperation with China is likely to be greater than its energy cooperation with the United States. According to the report, the countries of Central Asia give first priority to cooperation with their neighbors, which obviously puts the United States at a disadvantage. Furthermore, the location of the United States far from Central Asia would hamper efforts by the United States to use military force in the region.[8]

---

[7]James Hsiung, "China's Omni-Directional Diplomacy," *Asian Survey*, Vol. 35, No. 6, June 1995, pp. 573–586.

[8]Gu Guanfu, "Meiguo dui Zhongya de jieru yu Zhongguo anquan" ("U.S. Involvement in Central Asia and the Security of China"), in *Guoji xingshi fenxi baogao (Study Reports on the International Situation)*, Beijing: China Society for Strategy and Management Research, 1998, pp. 56–57.

The lack of a strong U.S. military presence in Central Asia explains China's enthusiasm for the proposed oil pipeline between China and Kazakhstan. The major attraction of this pipeline is that it would provide China with an oil supply route that avoids the sea-lanes dominated by the United States Navy and passes through regions where China's land power has the advantage.[9] Although many industry analysts immediately dismissed the pipeline as economically infeasible, it continues to appeal to a number of Chinese analysts and officials because it would help free China from dependency on oil controlled by an adversarial power in the event of a severe downturn in Sino-U.S. relations.[10]

China's interest in the development of Siberian energy resources can similarly be explained by their location in a region that is not dominated by U.S. military power. Proposed oil and gas pipelines, if constructed, would also provide China with an oil supply route free from the threat of the U.S. Navy. It should be noted, however, that this view is not uniformly held throughout the Chinese government. A number of China's leaders and People's Liberation Army officers reportedly are opposed to increasing energy cooperation with Russia on national security grounds. They are concerned that in the event of a Sino-Russian crisis, Russia would stop the flow of energy resources to China.[11]

The Chinese government wishes to reduce the vulnerability of its Middle Eastern oil supply to American power. China's leaders are uncomfortable with the fact that the United States is the preeminent power in the Middle East, the region that provides China with the bulk of its oil imports. Chinese energy security analysts point out that the United States controls access to oil in the Middle East and that Japan and the major European countries—allies of the United States—are large consumers of oil from this region. Despite the abundance of oil in the world today, these analysts perceive China to be in competition with the United States and its allies for Middle Eastern oil. They contend that China is at a disadvantage in this

---

[9]Zhang Wenmu, pp. 102–104.

[10]Robert S. Ross, "The Geography of the Peace: East Asia in the Twenty-First Century," *International Security*, Vol. 23, No. 4, Spring 1999, p. 108.

[11]Ögütçü, p. 137; Nixon.

"struggle" because China is not as influential in the region.[12] There is a concern that the United States, Japan, and the major European powers are apprehensive about China's entry into the ranks of those importing oil from the Middle East. Chinese analysts are afraid that these Western countries may seek to limit China's access to Middle East oil out of fear that there is not enough to go around.[13] This possible course of action is particularly troubling to China because its ties to Middle East oil producers are not as strong as are the ties of the United States and its allies. According to one analyst, "China was late in developing a strategy for establishing resource import relationships, and as a result, its relationships are not stable. This is especially true of those countries and territories from which China might import oil."[14] The Chinese government believes that the cultivation of strong bilateral relationships with oil-producing countries in the Middle East can help China secure the oil resources it needs from the region. China's efforts to establish closer ties with the Middle East have economic, political, and military dimensions.

Economically, China is pursuing what two analysts describe as a strategy of "two imports and one export" to strengthen its energy ties to the Middle East. The "two imports" refer to oil imports and capital to invest in the development of China's oil industry. Chinese oil companies have signed long-term supply contracts with Middle Eastern countries. For example, in May 1995, China negotiated with Iran to triple its oil imports from 20,000 b/d to 60,000 b/d. In October 1997, Saudi Aramco announced that China would also triple its crude imports from Saudi Arabia to 60,000 b/d.[15] The Chinese government has encouraged the participation of Middle Eastern oil companies in China's oil industry. As mentioned earlier, Saudi Aramco, the Kuwait Petroleum Corporation, and possibly the National Iranian Oil Company are upgrading and expanding China's

---

[12]Li Weijian, "Petroleum from the Middle East: China's Strategic Option in the 21st Century," *Zhongguo pinglun (China Review)*, No. 15, 3 March 1999, pp. 74–77, in FBIS (Document ID: FTS19990326000433); Wu Lei, p. 33.

[13]Wu Qiang and Xian Xuemei, "Zhongguo yu Zhongdong de nengyuan hezuo" ("China's Energy Cooperation with the Middle East"), *Zhanlue yu guanli (Strategy and Management)*, No. 2, 1999, p. 51.

[14]"Key Issues of Energy Development Strategy."

[15]John Calabrese, "China and the Persian Gulf: Energy and Security," *Middle East Journal*, Vol. 52, No. 3, Summer 1998, pp. 356–357.

refineries to process sour crudes from the Middle East. The "one export" refers to China's investment in oil exploration and development projects in the Middle East. In 1997, CNPC signed an agreement to develop and operate Iraq's al-Ahdab field. CNPC and CNOOC are also interested in investing in Iran. The Chinese government hopes that the development of strong Sino–Middle Eastern energy ties will help China secure the oil that it needs from this region.[16]

Politically, China is seeking to enhance the security of its oil imports from the Middle East by increasing its diplomacy in the region. The Chinese government appears to believe that strong bilateral political relationships can produce greater supply security during crises, despite historical evidence to the contrary. In 1999, several of China's top leaders visited Algeria, Israel, Jordan, Morocco, Saudi Arabia, and Syria—high-level visits to strengthen China's ties to states in a region where the U.S. has many allies and China has few. A recent report by the China Society for Strategy and Management Research suggests that this diplomacy may be successful with states unhappy with the American presence.[17] Indeed, China's closest bilateral relationships are with Iran and Iraq, the respective targets of UN and U.S. sanctions. It is likely that China's leaders view political support of these countries as a key measure to gain access to their energy supplies. China's permanent membership in the United Nations Security Council and its participation in the United Nations bodies dealing with sanctions were reportedly instrumental to China's success in its oil deal with Iraq.[18]

Militarily, it is possible that China could use its arms sales to the Middle East to foster closer ties to oil-producing nations and possibly to decrease its oil import bill.[19] China has a history of weapons ex-

---

[16]For more information on the "two imports, one export" strategy, see Wu Lei, pp. 32–33; and Shen Qinyu and Wu Lei.

[17]Wu Qiang and Xian Xuemei, p. 50.

[18]Sergei Troush, *China's Changing Oil Strategy and Its Foreign Policy Implications*, Center for Northeast Asian Policy Studies, Working Paper, Washington, DC: Brookings Institution, Fall 1999, www.brookings.edu/fp/cnaps/papers/1999_troush.html.

[19]Troush; Calabrese, p. 365; and Barry Rubin, "China's Middle East Strategy," *Middle East Review of International Affairs*, Vol. 3, No. 1, March 1999, www.biu.ac.il/SOC/besa/meria/journal/1999/issue1.

ports to Iran, Iraq, Libya, and Saudi Arabia. Of particular concern are China's sales to Iran of C-801 and C-802 antiship cruise missiles, which pose a threat to oil tanker traffic and American naval vessels in the Persian Gulf. Some Western analysts have speculated that despite China's September 1997 and January 1998 commitments to the United States to halt the export of antiship cruise missiles to Iran, arms-for-oil barter arrangements could still appeal to the Chinese government. Indeed, one analyst has speculated that NORINCO, a Chinese ordnance producer and major arms sales agent, is participating in the Chinese consortium formed to develop Iraq's al-Ahdab field to collect unpaid arms debts from the Iran-Iraq War.[20] Given the Chinese government's difficulties in collecting arms transfer payments from Iran, it is possible that China's leaders would consider exchanging arms for oil with Iran, especially when oil prices are high. There are, however, compelling reasons for the Chinese government not to continue selling antiship cruise missiles to Iran. First, Chinese officials may realize that Iran could use these weapons to interrupt the free flow of oil from this region. Second, U.S. officials consider Chinese cooperation on nonproliferation of weapons to be an important issue in Sino-U.S. relations, so that continued arms sales would strain China's relations with the country that is perceived to pose a great threat to China's energy security.

In short, the Chinese government hopes that the development of close relationships with oil-producing states in the Middle East can help China secure its fair share of oil from a region in which the United States is the preeminent power. China's economic, political, and military activities in the Middle East may facilitate investment there in oil exploration and development projects and the negotiation of long-term supply contracts with oil-producing states, particularly those at odds with the United States. However, increased Chinese involvement in the Middle East, in general, and its energy market, in particular, does not reduce the potential interference of the United States Navy with China's oil imports.

The corporate ambitions of CNPC, which are shared by the Chinese leadership, are also relevant to the Chinese government's efforts to decrease the vulnerability of its oil supply to American power.

---

[20]Email correspondence with oil industry analyst, 25 June 1999.

CNPC, not satisfied with being merely a state-owned enterprise, seeks to become a successful multinational corporation like Royal Dutch/Shell and Exxon-Mobil. The company's *1998 Annual Report* asserts, "Our mission is to join the ranks of the world famous petroleum companies."[21] CNPC president Ma Fucai intends for his company to rank "among the 10 leaders of the world's top 50 oil companies in terms of major economic quotas" by 2005.[22] Participation in the international oil market is essential to the achievement of this goal. CNPC's foreign investments give company officials the opportunity to prove they can do business overseas, learn the skills necessary to operate in a foreign environment, and gain exposure to new technology and management practices. In fact, the CNPC-owned China Petroleum Engineering and Construction Company so valued the opportunity to gain overseas work experience that they were willing to build a 940-mile pipeline and refinery in Sudan without a profit.[23] It is also likely that CNPC officials regard overseas deals as a way to enrich themselves personally from bribes and kickbacks.

The Chinese leadership supports CNPC's ambition to become a world-class oil company. The internationalization of CNPC is not only part of the Chinese government's plan to create internationally competitive firms but also its strategy to achieve energy security. The Chinese government appears to be uncomfortable with the dominance of the world oil market by companies from the United States, Japan, and Western Europe, allies that could potentially seek to limit China's access to oil.[24] It is likely that China's leaders regard the internationalization of CNPC as another way to ensure that China has access to the oil it needs. Furthermore, given the Chinese government's long-standing fear of dependency on foreign oil and its traditional need to control energy resources, the participation of Chinese oil companies in international oil exploration and develop-

---

[21]CNPC, *1998 Annual Report*, www.cnpc.com.cn. This statement is in the section on international cooperation.

[22]Li Wen, "Petroleum: Reorganization Promotes Development," *Beijing Review*, 2–8 November 1998, pp. 11–13.

[23]Ian Johnson, "China Cuts Sudan a Deal on Nile Oil Project," *Wall Street Journal*, 20 December 1999, p. A22.

[24]"Key Issues of Energy Development Strategy."

ment projects probably provides China's leaders with a measure of psychological security. There appears to be a perception among Chinese energy planners and analysts that equity holdings in overseas oil fields increase China's control over that imported oil. However, most of the oil produced by CNPC in places like Venezuela, Sudan, and Kazakhstan will not physically enter China because of logistical difficulties and transportation costs.

China's other energy security activities also seek, in part, to lessen the influence of the United States over China's energy supply. First, the Chinese government is attempting to reduce the amount of oil it has to import through increased domestic production. The involvement of foreign oil companies is essential to this goal because they possess the capital, technology, and large-project management skills that the Chinese companies lack and are necessary for exploration in promising but geologically complex areas. Second, the Chinese government seeks to reduce its oil imports through the development of China's natural gas industry. Although natural gas is generally regarded as a substitute for coal, it could be substituted for oil in the transportation sector. Natural-gas-driven vehicles are already used in several cities in China and may spread to others.[25] Finally, if China establishes a strategic petroleum reserve, it could deter short-term disruptions of China's oil supply. In fact, a strategic petroleum reserve would be a key measure in reducing China's energy vulnerability.

----

[25]Logan and Chandler, p. 41.

Chapter Five

CONCLUSION

China's energy security activities are a response to the country's growing need for foreign sources of energy. China's recent shift from a net oil exporter to a net oil importer is a matter of great concern to the Chinese leadership, who regard oil imports as a strategic vulnerability that could be exploited by foreign powers. The United States is currently the most powerful country in the world and is perceived by many in China as uncomfortable with China's rising power. As a result, the Chinese government views the United States as the primary threat to China's energy security. China's energy security activities reflect this concern; they are largely defensive and are designed to minimize the vulnerability of China's oil supply to American power. The Chinese government's keen interest in the development of Kazakhstan's oil reserves and the construction of a pipeline to transport oil from western Kazakhstan to western China can be explained by the desire of Chinese planners to secure an oil supply that avoids the American-controlled sea-lanes. Similarly, China's efforts to increase its economic, political, and possibly military ties to oil-producing states in the Middle East are aimed at securing access to oil from a region—where the United States is the preeminent military power—that provides China with the bulk of its oil imports. The internationalization of CNPC also reflects the desire of the Chinese government to gain a foothold in a world oil market where the leading companies belong to the United States and its allies. However, China's high-profile international energy security activities are unlikely to be effective at supply diversification or reduced vulnerability to American power. Not only is it doubtful that many of the proposed pipelines will be built, but China's overseas oil concessions probably will not yield enough oil to come close to matching China's needs over the next two decades. Furthermore, most of the oil produced in China's foreign concessions will not physically enter China because of transportation and logistical costs. The oil will most likely be sold on the international market or swapped for oil that will enter China. Consequently, China will remain reliant on U.S. protection of the sea-lanes for its energy (in)security.

BIBLIOGRAPHY

"A Slump in Oil Prices Badly Hits China," *Jingji ribao (Economic Daily)*, 21 May 1998, p. 7, in *World News Connection*, wnc.fedworld.gov (Document ID: 0evdnoa034864k).

Andrews-Speed, Philip, "China in Petroleum Politics," *Far Eastern Economic Review*, 14 May 1998, p. 37.

"Article Examines 21st Century Oil Strategy," *Liaowang (Outlook)*, No. 9, 3 March 1997, pp. 14–16, in James Mulvenon (ed.), *China Facts and Figures Annual Handbook*, Vol. 21, Gulf Breeze, FL: Academic International Press, 1997, pp. 272–276.

Baghdad Iraq Television Network, "Oil Contract Signed with China, Officials Comment," 4 June 1997, in *World News Connection*, wnc.fedworld.gov (Document ID: 0ebdi6100hgrzq).

Becquelin, Nicolas, "The Oil Industry in China Since the Reforms of the Open Door Policy," *China Perspectives*, No. 9, January/February 1997, pp. 21–31.

Behn, Sharon, "China, Kazakhstan Sign Deal for Huge Uzen Field," *Platt's Oilgram News*, Vol. 75, No. 186, 25 September 1997, p. 1.

_____, "CNPC Deal Tops $4 Billion," *Platt's Oilgram News*, Vol. 75, No. 108, 5 June 1997, p. 1.

Berkove, Daniel, and Ravid Haselkorn, "Asia Pacific Energy Investment in Central Asia: The Start of a New Trend?" *CERA Decision Brief*, February 1998.

Blagov, Sergei, "Russian Firms Resolve Siberia-PRC Oil Pipeline Dispute," *South China Morning Post*, 9 February 2000, p. 3.

_____, "Russia-Asia: Hard Times Aside, Moscow Still Eyes Gas Supply," *Interpress Service*, 31 May 1999.

Blumenthal, David, and Gray Sasser, "Fuel for the Next Century," *China Business Review*, Vol. 25, No. 4, July-August 1998, pp. 34–38.

British Petroleum Company, *BP Statistical Review of World Energy*, London, 1998.

Calabrese, John, "China and the Persian Gulf: Energy and Security," *Middle East Journal*, Vol. 52, No. 3, Summer 1998, pp. 351–366.

Calder, Kent, "Energy and Security in Northeast Asia's Arc of Crisis," in Michael Stankiewicz (ed.), *Energy Security in Northeast Asia: Fueling Security*, University of California Institute on Global Conflict and Cooperation, Policy Paper #35, February 1998, pp. 14–22.

_____, "Fueling the Rising Sun: Asia's Energy Needs and Global Security," *Harvard International Review*, Vol. 19, No. 3, Summer 1997, pp. 24–27, 68.

_____, *Pacific Defense: Arms, Energy, and America's Future in Asia*, New York: William Morrow and Company, Inc., 1996.

_____, "Asia's Empty Tank," *Foreign Affairs*, Vol. 75, No. 2, March/April 1996, pp. 55–69.

Chang Weimin, "Legislation Needed for Oil Reserve," *China Daily Business Weekly*, 8 June 1997, p. 1.

Chen Wenxian, "Jiang likely to bring home more crude from Saudi Arabia," *China Oil, Gas and Petrochemicals*, Vol. 7, No. 21, 1 November 1999, pp. 9–10, 13.

"China Exploring Overseas Petroleum Business," www.chinaeco.com, 8 September 1997.

"China Exports Oil from Sudan Project," www.chinaonline.com, 3 September 1999.

"China Leaps on to Global Oil Production Stage," *Petroleum Intelligence Weekly*, www.piwpubs.com, 9 June 1997.

"China National Offshore Oil to Reorganize," *Asian Wall Street Journal*, 6 January 1998, p. 4.

China National Petroleum Corporation, *1998 Annual Report*, www.cnpc.com.cn.

"China Stepping Up Foreign E&P Investment as Oil Imports Soar," *Oil & Gas Journal*, 9 May 1994, pp. 56–59.

"China Takes Control of Kazakhstan's Aktyubinsk," *East European Energy Report*, No. 69, 24 June 1997, p. 16.

"China to Import Crude, Not Products: Energy Security Analysis," *Asia Pulse*, 20 January 2000.

"China's CNPC and Shell to Co-develop Natural Gas Field," *Asia Pulse*, 20 March 2000.

"China's Guangdong Invites Bids for Liquefied Gas Project," *Asia Pulse*, 14 February 2000.

"China's Kazakh Oil Projects Hurt by Asian, Russian Financial Crises," *Iran News*, 11 October 1998.

"China's Oil Imports Rise, Possible Boon for US," *Oil & Gas Journal*, 7 June 1999, p. 24.

"China's Oil Price Reforms a Major Step in Deregulating Its Petroleum Sector," *Oil & Gas Journal*, 10 August 1998.

Christoffersen, Gaye, "China's Intentions for Russian and Central Asian Oil and Gas," *NBR Analysis*, Vol. 9, No. 2, March 1998.

Chu Shulong, "Sino-US Relations: The Necessity for Change and a New Strategy," *Contemporary International Relations*, Vol. 6, No. 11, November 1996, pp. 1–12.

Clover, Charles, "Kazakhs tread softly in the shadow of giant neighbor," *Financial Times*, 3 July 1999, p. 4.

_____, "Kazakhs and Chinese Press for Oil Deals," *Financial Times*, 6 July 1998, p. 4.

"CNPC Shelves China-Kazakhstan Oil Pipeline," *Oil & Gas Journal*, 30 August 1999, p. 44.

Corzine, Robert, "The Lure of the East: China, a Vast Potential Market for Kazakh Oil," *Financial Times*, 23 July 1997, p. 4.

Davis, Anthony, "China/Kazakhstan—Strategic Oil Deal Recently Completed," *Jane's Intelligence Review*, Vol. 4, No. 12, 1 December 1997, p. 9.

Dorian, James P., Brett Wigdortz, and Dru C. Gladney, "China and Central Asia's Volatile Mix: Energy, Trade, and Ethnic Relations," *Asia Pacific Issues*, No. 31, May 1997.

_____, "Central Asia and Xinjiang, China: Emerging Energy, Economic, and Ethnic Relations," *Central Asian Survey*, Vol. 16, No. 4, 1997, pp. 461–486.

Emergency Oil Stocks and Energy Security in the APEC Region, Tokyo, Japan: Asia Pacific Energy Research Centre, March 2000, www.ieej.or.jp/aperc/REPORTS.html.

"Energy: The New Oil Frontier," *China News Analysis*, No. 1611, 1 June 1998.

Fan Wenxin, "China's oil trade hits record highs in 1999," *China Oil, Gas and Petrochemicals*, Vol. 8, No. 3, 1 February 2000, pp. 10–13.

Fesharaki, Fereidun, "Oil Markets and Energy Security in Northeast Asia," in Michael Stankiewicz (ed.), *Energy Security in Northeast Asia: Fueling Security*, University of California Institute on Global Conflict and Cooperation, Policy Paper #35, February 1998, pp. 23–25.

Fesharaki, Fereidun, and Kang Wu, "Revitalizing China's Petroleum Industry through Reorganization: Will It Work?" *Oil & Gas Journal*, 10 August 1998.

_____, *Outlook for Energy Demand, Supply, and Government Policies in China*, Honolulu, Hawaii: East-West Center, 29 July 1998.

_____, *A Survey of Energy Investment Ties Between Asia and the Middle East*, Honolulu, Hawaii: East-West Center, June 1998.

_____, "Petroleum Links Between China and the Middle East: The Implications for U.S.-China Relations," *Energy Advisory*, No. 157, 25 July 1995.

Gong Zhengzheng, "Xinjiang Gas Heading to Shanghai," *China Daily Business Weekly*, 30 January 2000, p. 1.

Gu Guanfu, "Meiguo dui Zhongya de jieru yu Zhongguo anquan" ("US Involvement in Central Asia and the Security of China"), in *Guoji xingshi fenxi baogao (Study Reports on the International Situation)*, Beijing: China Society for Strategy and Management Research, 1998, pp. 52–58.

Gu Shuzhong, "PRC Resources Security Assessed," *Zhongguo kexue bao (China Science News)*, 2 December 1998, p. 3, in *World News Connection*, wnc.fedworld.gov (Document ID: 0f55msm01fsior).

Hafidh, Hassan, "Iraq and China Sign $1.2 Billion Oil Contract," Reuters World Service, 4 June 1997.

Holley, David, "China's Thirst for Oil Fuels Competition," *Los Angeles Times*, 28 July 1997, p. 1.

Hsiung, James, "China's Omni-Directional Diplomacy," *Asian Survey*, Vol. 35, No. 6, June 1995, pp. 573–586.

Huang Hong and Ji Ming, "United under the Great Banner of Patriotism—Thoughts on Strong Condemnations Against U.S.-Led Atrocities," *Renmin ribao (People's Daily)*, 27 May 1999, p. 9, in Foreign Broadcast Information Service (Document ID: FTS19990603002066).

"Islam and Oil Have China Thinking," *Washington Times*, 29 October 1997.

Jaffe, Amy Myers, and Robert A. Manning, "The Myth of the Caspian 'Great Game': The Real Geopolitics of Energy," *Survival*, Vol. 40, No. 4, Winter 1998–1999, pp. 112–129.

Ji Guoxing, "Yatai nengyuan anquan hezuo: xingshi yu renwu" ("Energy Security Cooperation in the Asia-Pacific Region: Situation and Mission"), *Guoji guancha (International Survey)*, No. 3, 1999, pp. 9–12.

Johnson, Ian, "China Cuts Sudan a Deal on Nile Oil Project," *Wall Street Journal*, 20 December 1999, p. A22.

_____, "For Chinese, Natural Gas Is Growing in Importance," *Wall Street Journal*, 26 August 1998, p. A19.

"Kao duoyuanhua baozhang Zhongguo youqi gongying" ("Rely on Diversification to Guarantee China's Oil and Gas Supply"), *Zhongguo shiyou bao (China Oil News)*, 12 January 2000, p. 1.

Keith, Ronald C., "China's 'Resource Diplomacy' and National Energy Policy," in Ronald C. Keith (ed.), *Energy Security and Economic Development in East Asia*, London: Croom Helm, 1986, pp. 17–78.

"Key Issues of Energy Development Strategy," *Guoji shangbao (International Business Daily)*, 14 July 1998, p. 6, in Foreign Broadcast Information Service (Document ID: FTS-19980925001692).

Knight, Jane, "The Bids Aren't Marginal on Day 2 in Venezuela," *Platt's Oilgram News*, Vol. 75, No. 107, p. 1.

"Kogas to Take Part in Gas Pipeline Construction Project Linking Kovyktinskoye Gas Field to China," *Russian Oil and Gas Report*, 11 October 1999.

Krekel, Bryan A., "Cross-Border Trade and Ethnic Unrest in Xinjiang: Conflict and Cooperation in the Origins of Chinese-Kazakh Energy Relations," unpublished M.A. thesis, University of Washington, 1998.

Lee, Winnie, "CNPC's Spree Looks to Fill Supply Gap," *Platt's Oilgram News*, Vol. 75, No. 165, 26 August 1997, p. 1.

_____, "China Firm Begins Sudan Work in March," *Platt's Oilgram News*, Vol. 75, No. 25, 5 February 1997, p. 3.

Leung, Julia, "China Takes Risk in Policy on Oil Basins," *Asian Wall Street Journal*, 27 May 1991.

Li Peng, "China's Policy on Energy Resources," *Xinhua*, 28 May 1997, in *World News Connection*, wnc.fedworld.gov (Document ID: drchi119-n-97001).

Li Shulong, "Di san zhi yan kan Zhongguo shiyou" ("The Third Eye Looks at China's Oil"), *Zhongguo shiyou bao (China Oil News)*, 18 January 2000, p. 2.

Li Weijian, "Petroleum from the Middle East: China's Strategic Option in the 21st Century," *Zhongguo pinglun (China Review)*, No. 15, 3 March 1999, pp. 74–77, in Foreign Broadcast Information Service (Document ID: FTS19990326000433).

Li Wen, "Petroleum: Reorganization Promotes Development," *Beijing Review*, 2–8 November 1998, pp. 11–13.

Lieberthal, Kenneth, *Governing China: From Revolution to Reform*, New York: W. W. Norton & Company, 1995.

Lieberthal, Kenneth, and Michel Oksenberg, *Policy Making in China: Leaders, Structures, and Processes*, Princeton: Princeton University Press, 1988.

Liesman, Steve, "Russia-to-China Natural Gas Pipeline Is Agreed Upon at Yeltsin-Jiang Summit," *Wall Street Journal*, 11 November 1997, p. A14.

Lin Ye and Zhang Zhong, "Models of Development and Trends in Investment for Multinational Oil Companies," *Guoji maoyi (Intertrade)*, 20 August 1997, pp. 29–31, in Foreign Broadcast Information Service (Document ID: FTS19971008000597).

Liu Jiangyong, "Xin 'RiMei fangwei hezuo zhizhen' yu ZhongRi guanxi" ("New 'Guidelines for Japanese-U.S. Cooperative Defense' and Sino-Japanese Relations"), in *Guoji xingshi fenxi baogao (Study Reports on the International Situation)*, Beijing: China Society for Strategy and Management Research, 1998, pp. 18–26.

Logan, Jeffrey and William Chandler, "Natural Gas Gains Momentum," *China Business Review*, Vol. 25, No. 4, July-August 1998, pp. 40–45.

Ma Hong and Sun Zhu, "Jianli woguo zhanlue shiyou chubei de zhengshi kaolü" ("Thoughts on Establishing China's Strategic Petroleum Reserve"), *Zhanlue yu guanli (Strategy and Management)*, No. 1, 1997, pp. 46–51.

Ma Xiuqing, "Zhongguo de shiyou jinkou xuyao he tong Alabo guojia shiyou hezuo de fazhan" ("China's Demand for Oil Imports and the Development of Its Cooperation with Arab Oil-Producing States"), *Xiya Feizhou (West Asia and Africa)*, No. 2, 1997, pp. 16–21.

Maddison, Angus, *Chinese Economic Performance in the Long Run*, Paris: Organization for Economic Cooperation and Development, 1998.

May, Michael, *Energy and Security in East Asia*, Stanford, CA: Institute for International Studies, Stanford University, January 1998.

McDonald, Paul, "China: is the 'open door' about to close?" *World Today*, Vol. 57, No. 7, July 1995, pp. 145–148.

Munro, Ross, "Chinese Energy Strategy," in *Energy Strategies and Military Strategies in Asia*, McLean, VA: Hicks & Associates, September 1999, Appendix G.

"Natural Gas to Power More Cars," www.chinaeco.com, 28 September 1998.

Nixon, Malcolm, "BP-Amoco—Wrong Footed Again?" *Hart's Asian Petroleum News*, Vol. 3, No. 43, 1 November 1999.

O'Brien, Dennis, "Mightier than the Sword: Energy Markets and Global Security," *Harvard International Review*, Vol. 19, No. 3, Summer 1997, pp. 8–11, 62–63.

Ögütçü, Mehmet, "China's Energy Future and Global Implications," in Werner Draguhn and Robert Ash (eds.), *China's Economic Security*, New York: St. Martin's Press, 1999, pp. 84–141.

"Oil Security Risk, Wolf at Door?" *China Oil, Gas and Petrochemicals*, Vol. 5, No. 10, 15 May 1997, pp. 1–5.

O'Neill, Mark, "Hopes Fade of an Uighur Homeland," *South China Morning Post*, 21 June 1999, p. 17.

Ottaway, David B., and Dan Morgan, "China Pursues Ambitious Role in Oil Market," *Washington Post*, 26 December 1997, p. 1.

Paik, Keun-Wook, *Gas and Oil in Northeast Asia: Policies, Projects, and Prospects*, London: Royal Institute of International Affairs, 1995.

Paik, Keun-Wook, and Jae-Yong Choi, "Pipeline Gas Trade Between Asia and Russia, Northeast Asia Gets a Fresh Look," *Oil & Gas Journal*, 18 August 1997, p. 41.

Park, Choon-ho, and Jerome Alan Cohen, "The Politics of the Oil Weapon," *Foreign Policy*, No. 20, Fall 1975, pp. 28–40.

"PRC, Saudi Arabia to Build Refinery in Fujian," *Wen wei po*, 3 November 1999, p. A2, in Foreign Broadcast Information Service (Document ID: FTS19991103000187).

Quan Lan, "Sino-foreign onshore cooperation after IPO," *China Oil, Gas and Petrochemicals*, Vol. 8, No. 8, 15 April 2000, p. 3.

———, "Transnational oil pipeline shelved," *China Oil, Gas and Petrochemicals*, Vol. 7, No. 16, 15 August 1999, pp. 2–3.

Quan Lan and Keun-Wook Paik, *China Natural Gas Report*, London: Royal Institute of International Affairs, 1998.

Rashid, Ahmed, and Trish Saywell, "Beijing Gusher, China Pays Hugely to Bag Energy Supplies Abroad," *Far Eastern Economic Review*, 26 February 1998, pp. 46–48.

Ren Rouen, *China's Economic Performance in an International Perspective*, Paris: Organization for Economic Cooperation and Development, 1997.

"Resource Warriors," *Asian Wall Street Journal*, 23 July 1997, p. 8.

Ross, Robert S., "The Geography of the Peace: East Asia in the Twenty-First Century," *International Security*, Vol. 23, No. 4, Spring 1999, pp. 81–118.

Rubin, Barry, "China's Middle East Strategy," *Middle East Review of International Affairs*, Vol. 3, No. 1, March 1999, www.biu.ac.il/ SOC/besa/meria/journal/1999/issue1.

Ruseckas, Laurent, "State of the Field Report: Energy and Politics in Central Asia and the Caucasus," http://204.201.190.101/products/aareview/Vol1/No2/essay1.html.

"Russia to increase oil supplies to China," *Moscow Interfax*, 7 September 1999, in *World News Connection*, wnc.fedworld.gov (Document ID: 0fhssxc041212p).

Salameh, Mamdouh G., "The Geopolitics of Oil in the Asia-Pacific Region and Its Strategic Implications," *OPEC Review*, Vol. 21, No. 2, June 1997, pp. 125–131.

_____, "China, Oil and the Risk of Regional Conflict," *Survival*, Vol. 37, No. 4, Winter 1995–1996, pp. 133–146.

Saywell, Trish, and Ahmed Rashid, "Innocent Abroad," *Far Eastern Economic Review*, 26 February 1998, p. 50.

Shen Qinyu and Wu Lei, "Focus on the Gulf Region in Developing Oil Industry," *Guoji maoyi wenti (International Trade Journal)*, No. 2, 6 February 1995, pp. 9–12, in *World News Connection*, wnc.fedworld.gov (Document ID: 0di1s8r002sg6p).

Stephan, Katherine, "Big Gusher," *China Trade Report*, Vol. 36, June 1998.

"Sudan Deal Signed by Arakis, Government, and Partners," *Platt's Oilgram News*, Vol. 75, No. 43, 4 March 1997, p. 1.

"Sudan Pipeline Operational," *Petroleum Economist*, 26 August 1999, p. 15.

Sun Tan, "Mei dui Hua 'nengyuan ezhi' bu neng decheng" ("America's 'Energy Containment Policy' Against China Will Not Succeed"), *Zhongguo kuangye bao (China Mining News)*, 15 December 1999, p. 3.

Szulc, Tad, "The New Bigfoot in the Global Oil Market," *Los Angeles Times*, 5 October 1997, p. 2.

Tansey, Robert, "Black Gold Rush," *China Business Review*, Vol. 21, No. 4, July–August 1994, pp. 8–16.

"Tehran Presses Beijing on Neka-Tehran Bid," *Hart's Asian Petroleum News*, Vol. 4, No. 4, 31 January 2000.

Troush, Sergei, *China's Changing Oil Strategy and Its Foreign Policy Implications*, Center for Northeast Asian Policy Studies, Working Paper, Washington, DC: Brookings Institution, Fall 1999, www.brookings.edu/fp/cnaps/papers/1999_troush.html.

United States Energy Information Administration, "Sudan," www.eia.doe.gov, November 1999.

_____, "China: An Energy Sector Overview," www.eia.doe.gov, October 1997.

_____, "East Asia: The Energy Situation," www.eia.doe.gov, February 1998.

_____, *International Energy Outlook 1998*, Washington, DC: Government Printing Office, April 1998.

_____, *International Energy Outlook 1999*, Washington, DC: Government Printing Office, April 1999.

_____, "Iraq," www.eia.doe.gov, November 1998.

Upperton, Jane, and Sharon Behn, "China-Kazakh Line Is Open to 'Outsiders,'" *Platt's Oilgram News*, Vol. 75, No. 192, 3 October 1997, p. 3.

Valencia, Mark J., "Energy and Insecurity in Asia," *Survival*, Vol. 39, No. 3, Autumn 1997, pp. 85–106.

Valencia, Mark J., and James P. Dorian, "Multilateral Cooperation in Northeast Asia's Energy Sector: Possibilities and Problems," in Michael Stankiewicz (ed.), *Energy and Security in Northeast Asia: Supply and Demand; Conflict and Cooperation*, University of California Institute on Global Conflict and Cooperation, Policy Paper #36, February 1998, pp. 41–58.

Wimbush, S. Enders, *China Futures Workshop Final Report*, SAIC Document No. 01-1175-04-7048-000, 17 December 1996.

Woodward, Kim, *The International Energy Relations of China*, Stanford, CA: Stanford University Press, 1980.

World Bank, "Country Brief: China," worldbank.org, June 1998.

_____, *China 2020: Development Challenges in the New Century*, Washington, DC, 1997.

Wu Lei, "Zhongdong shiyou yu woguo weilai shiyou gongqiu pingheng" ("Middle East Oil and Our Equilibrium of Oil Supply and Demand in the Future"), *Shijie jingji yu zhengzhi (World Economics and Politics)*, No. 3, 1997, pp. 30–33.

Wu Qiang and Xian Xuemei, "Zhongguo yu Zhongdong de nengyuan hezuo" ("China's Energy Cooperation with the Middle East"), *Zhanlue yu guanli (Strategy and Management)*, No. 2, 1999, pp. 49–52.

Xiao Feng, "Views on Some Hot-Spot Issues in International Situation," *Xiandai guoji guanxi (Contemporary International Relations)*, No. 12, December 1999, pp. 1–5, in Foreign Broadcast Information Service (Document ID: FTS20000212000168).

Xinhua, "PRC Sees Natural Gas as Supplement to Petroleum," 16 October 1997, in *World News Connection*, wnc.fedworld.gov (Document ID: 0eih70r03suv37).

_____, "Experts Call for a Pan-Asian Oil Bridge," 16 June 1996, in *World News Connection*, wnc.fedworld.gov (Document ID: 0dt7tt303s348w).

Xu Xiaojie, "The Oil and Gas Linkages Between Central Asia and China: A Geopolitical Perspective," Baker Institute Working Paper, Houston, Texas: Rice University, April 1998.

_____, *Xin shiji de youqi diyuan zhengzhi: Zhongguo mianlin de jiyu yu tiaozhan* ("The Geopolitics of Oil and Gas in the New Century: The Opportunities and Challenges Facing China"), Beijing: Social Science Literature Press, April 1998.

_____, "China Reaches Crossroads for Strategic Choices," *World Oil*, Vol. 28, No. 4, April 1997, pp. 95–100.

Xu Yihe, "China's Dependence on the Middle East May Increase," *Asian Wall Street Journal*, 30 March 1999, p. 25.

Yan Xuetong, "China's Strategic Security Environment," *Shijie zhishi (World Affairss)*, No. 3, February 2000, pp. 8–10, in Foreign Broadcast Information Service (Document ID: FTS2000021600038).

_____, "Zhongguo fazhan miandui de guoji anquan huanjing" ("The International Security Environment that Faces China's Development"), in *Guoji xingshi fenxi baogao (Study Reports on the International Situation)*, Beijing: China Society for Strategy and Management Research, 1998, pp. 4–9.

Yang Qing, "Yao cong zhanlue gaodu zhongshi LNG jinkou" ("Pay Attention to LNG Imports in High-Level Strategy"), *Zhongguo nengyuan (Energy of China)*, No. 5, 1998, pp. 5–8.

Yatsko, Pamela, "Oh Well, China's Tarim Basin Is Proving a Big Disappointment," *Far Eastern Economic Review*, 19 September 1996, pp. 68–69.

Yergin, Daniel, Dennis Eklof, and Jefferson Edwards, "Fueling Asia's Recovery," *Foreign Affairs*, Vol. 77, No. 2, March/April 1998, pp. 34–50.

"Yukos to Organize Consortium for Construction of Oil Pipeline to China," *Russian Oil and Gas Report*, 31 March 2000.

Zhang Wenmu, "Meiguo de shiyou diyuan zhanlue yu Zhongguo Xizang Xinjiang diqu anquan ("U.S. Petroleum Geography Strategy and the Security of Tibet and Xinjiang"), *Zhanlue yu guanli (Strategy and Management)*, No. 2, 1998, pp. 100–104.

Zhang Yirong, "China Quickens Its Pace of Overseas Oil Operation," *China Oil & Gas*, Vol. 4, No. 3, September 1997, p. 174.

Zhao Hongtu and Li Rong, "Jianli woguo zhanlue shiyou chubei shizai bixing" ("Need for China to Establish Strategic Petroleum Reserves"), *Guoji shiyou jingji (International Petroleum Economics)*, Vol. 7, No. 2, March 1999, pp. 24–28, 56.

Zhao Shaoqin, "Reviving Oil Market Restores Confidence," *China Daily Business Weekly*, 16 August 1998, p. 1.

Zhao Yining and Pu Shurou, "Zhongguo shiyou mianlin de tiaozhan" ("The Challenges Facing Chinese Oil"), *Liaowang (Outlook)*, No. 9, 3 March 1997, pp. 10–14.